Laurence Yep

WHO WROTE THAT?

LOUISA MAY ALCOTT

JANE AUSTEN

AVI

JUDY BLUME

BETSY BYARS

BEVERLY CLEARY

ROBERT CORMIER

BRUCE COVILLE

ROALD DAHL

CHARLES DICKENS

THEODOR GEISEL

WILL HOBBS

ANTHONY HOROWITZ

GAIL CARSON LEVINE

C.S. LEWIS

ANN M. MARTIN

L.M. MONTGOMERY

PAT MORA

WALTER DEAN MYERS

SCOTT O'DELL

BARBARA PARK

GARY PAULSEN

TAMORA PIERCE

EDGAR ALLAN POE

BEATRIX POTTER

PHILIP PULLMAN

MYTHMAKER:
   THE STORY
    OF J.K. ROWLING

MAURICE SENDAK

SHEL SILVERSTEIN

R.L. STINE

EDWARD L.
   STRATEMEYER

E.B. WHITE

LAURA INGALLS
   WILDER

LAURENCE YEP

JANE YOLEN

WHO WROTE THAT?

Laurence Yep

Hal Marcovitz

Foreword by
Kyle Zimmer

CHELSEA HOUSE
PUBLISHERS
An imprint of Infobase Publishing

Laurence Yep

Chelsea House
An imprint of Infobase Publishing
132 West 31st Street
New York NY 10001

Library of Congress Cataloging-in-Publication Data
Marcovitz, Hal.
　Laurence Yep / Hal Marcovitz.
　　　p. cm. — (Who wrote that?)
　Includes bibliographical references and index.
　ISBN 978-0-7910-9527-0 (hardcover)
　1. Yep, Laurence—Juvenile literature. 2. Authors, American—20th century—
Biography—Juvenile literature. 3. Authors, American—21st century—Biography—
Juvenile literature. 4. Young adult fiction—Authorship—Juvenile literature. 5.
Chinese Americans—Biography—Juvenile literature. I. Title. II. Series.
　PS3575.E6Z79 2008
　813'.54—dc22
　[B]　　　　　　　　　　　2007045508

Text design by Keith Trego and Erika K. Arroyo
Cover design by Keith Trego and Jooyoung An

Printed in the United States of America

Bang EJB 10 9 8 7 6 5 4 3 2 1

This book is printed on acid-free paper.

Table of Contents

FOREWORD BY
KYLE ZIMMER
PRESIDENT, FIRST BOOK

HUMANITY IS POWERED by stories. From our earliest days as thinking beings, we employed every available tool to tell each other stories. We danced, drew pictures on the walls of our caves, spoke, and sang. All of this extraordinary effort was designed to entertain, recount the news of the day, explain natural occurrences—and then gradually to build religious and cultural traditions and establish the common bonds and continuity that eventually formed civilizations. Stories are the most powerful force in the universe; they are the primary element that has distinguished our evolutionary path.

Our love of the story has not diminished with time. Enormous segments of societies are devoted to the art of storytelling. Book sales in the United States alone topped $26 billion last year; movie studios spend fortunes to create and promote stories; and the news industry is more pervasive in its presence than ever before.

There is no mystery to our fascination. Great stories are magic. They can introduce us to new cultures or remind us of the nobility and failures of our own; inspire us to greatness or scare us to death; but above all, stories provide human insight on a level that is unavailable through any other source. In fact, stories connect each of us to the rest of humanity not just in our own time, but also throughout history.

This special magic of books is the greatest treasure that we can hand down from generation to generation. In fact, that spark in a child that comes from books became the motivation for the creation of my organization, First Book, a national literacy program with a simple mission: to provide new books to the most disadvantaged children. First Book has been at work in hundreds of communities for over a decade. Every year, children in need receive millions of books through our organization, and millions more are provided through dedicated literacy institutions across the United States and around the world. In addition, groups of people dedicate themselves tirelessly to working with children to share reading and stories in every imaginable setting from schools to the streets. Of course, this Herculean effort serves many important goals. Literacy translates to productivity and employability in life and many other valid and even essential elements. But at the heart of this movement are people who love stories, love to read, and want desperately to ensure that no one misses the wonderful possibilities that reading provides.

When thinking about the importance of books, there is an overwhelming urge to cite the literary devotion of great minds. Some have written of the magnitude of the importance of literature. Amy Lowell, an American poet, captured the concept when she said, "Books are more than books. They are the life, the very heart and core of ages past, the reason why men lived and worked and died, the essence and quintessence of their lives." Others have spoken of their personal obsession with books, as in Thomas Jefferson's simple statement: "I live for books." But more compelling, perhaps, is the almost instinctive excitement in children for books and stories.

Throughout my years at First Book, I have heard truly extraordinary stories about the power of books in the lives of children. In one case, a homeless child, who had been bounced from one location to another, later resurfaced—and the only possession that he had fought to keep was the book he was given as part of a First Book distribution months earlier. More recently, I met a child who, upon receiving the book he wanted, flashed a big smile and said, "This is my big chance!" These snapshots reveal the true power of books and stories to give hope and change lives.

As these children grow up and continue to develop their love of reading, they will owe a profound debt to those volunteers who reached out to them—a debt that they may repay by reaching out to spark the next generation of readers. But there is a greater debt owed by all of us—a debt to the storytellers, the authors, who have bound us together, inspired our leaders, fueled our civilizations, and helped us put our children to sleep with their heads full of images and ideas.

WHO WROTE THAT? is a series of books dedicated to introducing us to a few of these incredible individuals. While we have almost always honored stories, we have not uniformly honored storytellers. In fact, some of the most important authors have toiled in complete obscurity throughout their lives or have been openly persecuted for the uncomfortable truths that they have laid before us. When confronted with the magnitude of their written work, we can forget that writers are people. They struggle through the same daily indignities and dental appointments, and they experience the intense joy and bottomless despair that many of us do. Yet, somehow they rise above it all to weave a powerful thread that connects us all. It is a rare honor to have the opportunity that these books provide to share the lives of these extraordinary people. Enjoy.

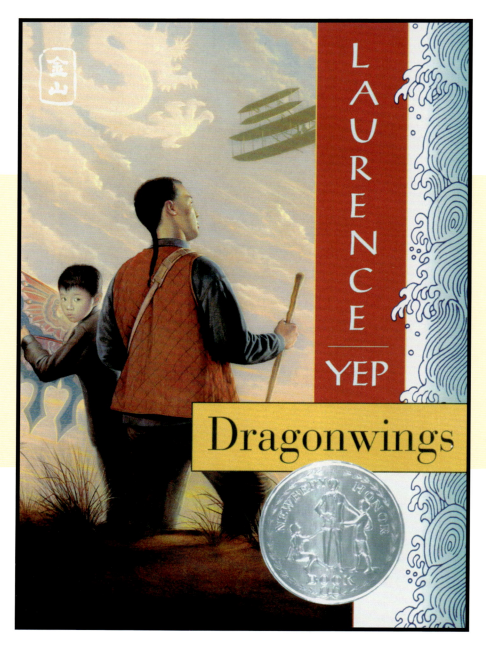

In writing **Dragonwings,** *Laurence Yep modeled the main character on a real-life person, Fung Joe Guey, a Chinese-American man who experimented with powered flight in the early 1900s.*

1

A Novelist Takes Wing

STUDENTS OF AVIATION history know that Wilbur and Orville Wright made the first flight in an engine-powered airplane over a sandy North Carolina beach in 1903. Much more obscure, however, is the story of Fung Joe Guey, a Chinese-American man who experimented with powered flight. He flew for 20 minutes in a biplane of his own design near Oakland, California, in 1909.

Years later, author Laurence Yep discovered Fung's story in some old newspaper clippings. After he researched the story, Yep wrote *Dragonwings*, a fictional account of the flight that centers on Moon Shadow, a character modeled on Fung. In the book, Moon Shadow leaves China for California, where he joins his father and helps him establish a home for the rest of their family. Together, Moon Shadow and his father, whom Yep has named Windrider, pursue their dream to build and fly an airplane.

When Yep came across Fung's story, he was an English professor at San Jose City College in California. He had been writing for many years and had published several short stories and the novel *Sweetwater*. *Dragonwings* would turn out to be a much different type of project for Yep. Until then, most of his work had been in the genre of science fiction. (*Sweetwater* tells the story of a clash between alien races on a distant planet.) Yep intended *Dragonwings* to be a work of historical fiction, which means it would be a fictional story based on a true episode from history.

Yep had little experience as a writer of historical fiction. Indeed, as Yep started to research Fung's story, he discovered how little he knew about the first Chinese immigrants in America, even though he had grown up in a Chinese-American home in San Francisco. Yep recalled, "I had grown up as a child in the 1950s so that my sense of reality was an American one. Now I had to grow up again, but this time in the 1900s, developing a Chinese sense of reality."[1]

Yep learned that people emigrated from China to America for the same reason that people emigrated from Europe: Many of them lived in poverty or under despotic rulers. People also fled their homeland to escape the warfare that plagued China during the 1800s and 1900s. The Chinese called America the "Golden Mountain." Like the Europeans who flooded across the Atlantic Ocean, the Chinese believed that America was the land of freedom and opportunity.

The Chinese-American community in the late 1800s and 1900s was a bachelor society, which means that most of the immigrants were men. It was unusual for the men to have enough money to buy passage for their wives and children, so they made the voyage alone while other family members typically stayed behind in China. Once they arrived in America, the men hoped to be able to find jobs and save enough money to buy steamship passage for their loved ones.

Unfortunately, things were not that simple. In America, Chinese immigrants faced racism and hostility from many Americans who believed the Chinese would take their jobs. In 1882, Congress adopted the Chinese Exclusion Act, which remained a federal law until it was finally repealed in 1943. This act specified that only immigrants with a parent who was a citizen of the United States would be permitted to enter. Immigration officers interrogated Chinese immigrants and investigated their claims that their mothers or fathers had gained American citizenship. Officials often held them at the immigration station on Angel Island in San Francisco Bay for weeks or months at a time.

Moon Shadow met this fate in 1903, when he arrived at Angel Island. In *Dragonwings*, Yep describes the interrogation that eight-year-old Moon Shadow undergoes by the white immigration officers, whom the boy calls "demons." Says Moon Shadow,

> The demons kept us locked inside a long, two-story warehouse for a week before it was our turn to be questioned. I don't like to think about it too much. We were kept on the bottom story, where we slept and ate off the floors. All the time, we smelled the sewage and the bilge of the bay—besides which there was no way to bathe there, so after the long boat voyage, we were rather a fragrant group on our own.

Finally, though, when the demons called me for questioning, I found they already had a big bunch of papers on my father. Inside it was the record of his first interview, which ran for some one hundred and fifty pages. They spent an hour looking at it and then asking me questions about my village and kinsmen. They tried to trip me up so they could prove I was not my father's son, but they did not succeed.[2]

As Yep developed the characters of Moon Shadow and Windrider, he learned that there was little information available on the more than 175,000 Chinese immigrants who arrived in San Francisco in the late 1800s and early 1900s. Who were these people? What were their talents? Were they craftsmen? Yep found that the record was painfully thin and provided few details about the individuals who had done so much to form the vibrant Chinese-American community of San Francisco. Yep explained, "Trying to research Chinese American history—that is, the history of men and women of Chinese ancestry who had been influenced by their experiences of America—can be difficult. . . . It took some six years of research in the libraries of different cities to find the bits and pieces that could be fitted into Chinese American history."[3]

During his research, Yep found himself surprisingly ignorant of his own heritage and Chinese culture. Because he was raised Catholic, Yep had to learn about the traditional religions of his homeland, as well as the cultural practices and rites practiced by the Chinese. For example, early in *Dragonwings*, Moon Shadow explains that a Chinese man

can have several names. He has a family name and a personal name given to him at birth. He can have another name given to him when he comes of age, a nickname from his friends, and if he is a poet, he can have a pen name. We are not like

Did you know...

Laurence Yep has written plays in addition to novels. An adaptation of *Dragonwings* has been performed on stage at Kennedy Center in Washington and at Lincoln Center in New York, as well as by dozens of regional children's theater companies.

"It was both interesting and challenging to adapt my novel for a different medium," Yep said. "The delightful part was being able to watch the faces of the audience in the theater because I cannot see my readers' reactions when they read my books."*

Before he adapted *Dragonwings*, Yep had written two one-act plays, *Pay the Chinaman* and *Fairy Bones*, both of which have been produced in New York and San Francisco.

Yep's wife, author Joanne Ryder, said, "It is always more lively around the house when Larry is involved with a play. Working in the theater is more social and collaborative than working in publishing. We've learned to expect and chuckle at the phone calls from actors querying their motivation and questioning their lines. When Larry writes books, he might wake up thinking about his characters, but they don't phone at midnight."**

* Quoted in Laurence Yep, "Hyperion Books for Children Biography," www.hyperionbooksforchildren.com/authors/displayAI.asp?id=191&ai=a.

** Joanne Ryder, "Laurence Yep," *Horn Book* 81, no. 4 (July–August 2005): p. 433.

the demons, who lock a child into one name from birth—with maybe a nickname if he is lucky. We feel that a man should be able to change his name as he changes, the way a hermit crab can throw away his shell when it's too small and find another one.[4]

In the story, Moon Shadow's father has taken the name Windrider because of his skill as a kite builder. In fact, when the boy arrives in San Francisco, his father gives him the gift of a beautiful kite shaped like a butterfly.

The relationship between Windrider and Moon Shadow is at the heart of the story. At first, the boy and his father are strangers, who meet for the first time when Moon Rider is released from the immigration station. Windrider is a warm, loving man who believes that hard work and ingenuity will help him overcome the obstacles and carve out a home in America for himself and his family. Yep based Windrider's character on his own father, Thomas Yep, a hardworking San Francisco grocery store owner. He was also a kite maker, and some of his kites were fashioned to resemble butterflies. Yep said of his father, "With his feet planted firmly in the grass and with just a puff of breeze, he could coax a kite up high into the sky."[5]

Of course, the climax of *Dragonwings* occurs when Windrider and Moon Shadow launch Windrider's biplane. At this point, the book has covered six years in the lives of the two characters. Moon Shadow is now a teenager who has endured racism, but he has learned that not all white people are demons. In fact, he has become close friends with a young white girl named Robin. Moon Shadow has also grown close to his father, and he and Robin help Windrider launch the biplane, which they have named "Dragonwings":

In researching Fung Joe Guey's story, Yep learned a great deal about the history of Chinese immigrants in the United States, which set him on a new path: writing historical fiction. Among the things he learned was the story of the Angel Island Immigration Station in California (above), which processed one million immigrants from 1910 to 1940.

Suddenly the wind blew even harder up the hillside. The grass all over the hill hissed even louder, like one giant snake. The nose of Dragonwings suddenly tilted up like some bird scenting the wind that would carry it home. The wind roared over the hilltop, seeming to gather beneath the wings. The canvas of the wings bellied upward, taut and swollen and eager. Dragonwings seemed to leap into the air about five feet and hang suspended. I held my breath. I saw Father twist his hips to the right, and the wings began to curl and the rear rudder curved to the right. Slowly, ever so slowly, Father began to bank in that direction. He had controlled flight! He was free in the sky.[6]

Dragonwings was enormously successful. Published in 1975, Yep's second novel established him as an important voice in young people's literature, particularly as an author of historical fiction. Critics praised the novel. *New York Times* book critic Ruth H. Pelmas declared *Dragonwings* "an exquisitely written poem of praise to the courage and industry of the Chinese American people."[7] Indeed, a year after its publication, the American Library Association selected *Dragonwings* as a Newbery Honor Book, which is one of the highest awards for young people's literature in the United States.

Yep did not conclude Moon Shadow's story with *Dragonwings*. He wrote eight more books about Moon Shadow and his family, in a series he called the "Golden Mountain Chronicles." The books trace the history of Windrider's family over a period of some 150 years. Yep recalls,

> I had wanted to write a story based on a real-life Chinese American aviator. However, I had to put him in his proper context which was the Chinatown of the 1900s. In the Chinatown I had known as a child, everyone knew one another; and the same thing happened in my fictional Chinatown. He kept introducing me to friends and family until I wound up writing about seven generations and covered 150 years of American history.[8]

In the years since then, Yep has written more than 60 novels and other types of literature. Although his books have different styles and include science fiction and fantasy, mystery and suspense, and contemporary dramas of life in America, he believes there is at least one theme that is common in all of his work: With imagination, all people can overcome obstacles. "When I wrote of the aeroplane, called 'Dragonwings,' I was actually dealing with the reach of our imagination," Yep said. "Windrider and his son, Moon Shadow, are engaged not only in the process of discovering America and each other, but also in a pilgrimage, or even a quest for a special moment when they can reaffirm the power of the imagination; that power in each of us to grasp with the mind and heart what we cannot immediately grasp with the hand."[9]

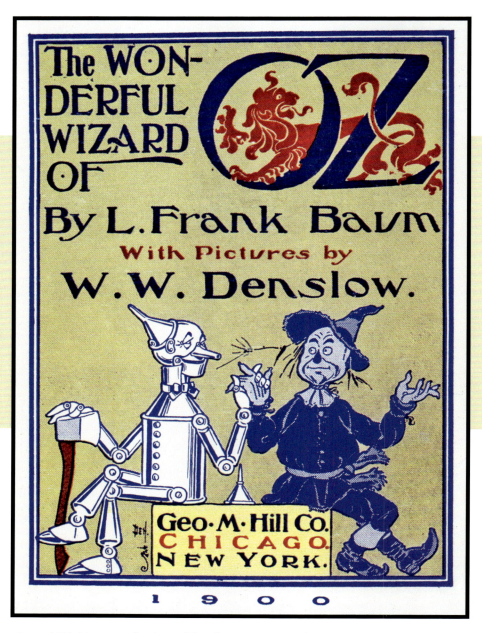

As a child, Yep was fascinated by the Oz series, which was based on The Wonderful Wizard of Oz by L. Frank Baum. The books, which featured fantastic creatures like witches, Munchkins, and flying monkeys, influenced Yep greatly.

2

An Outsider Becomes a Writer

WHEN LAURENCE YEP recalls his childhood, he thinks mostly about the familiar aromas from his parents' grocery store on Pierce Street in San Francisco. "The one thing that ruled my family's lives was our grocery store," he said.

> Even today, if I smell old plaster, I feel almost as if I am in the back in our old storeroom where the plaster was crumbling off the wooden laths. Or if I smell the coppery odor of liver, I think of washing out the bloody porcelain pan in which we used to display that kind of meat. If I smell old dollar bills, I can imagine myself back in the dark, quiet store, helping my mother put away the day's receipts.[1]

Yep and his family lived in an apartment above the store. Each morning, seven days a week, his parents would make their way downstairs to open the store for business. As a precaution against robbery, Yep's mother, Franche, always walked down the back steps with the money for the cash register; she would then enter the store from an inside door. His father, Thomas, opened the front door of the store from the street and picked up the bundles of newspapers that the delivery trucks left on the curb out front.

As boys, Laurence and his older brother Tom both worked in the store. Laurence worked behind the counter (he once admitted to being cheated out of candy bars by a young girl who paid him with the same nickel over and over again), but his main job was to restock the shelves. Dozens of products, such as vegetables, cereals, soft drinks, and canned goods, had to be constantly placed and replaced on the shelves in the store. He said, "At the base of the shelves on the western wall were bins. In those, we put cans of soup, laying them in rows on their sides. I got fairly good at juggling them, tossing one marked can from my right hand to my left. As my left hand put the can on the shelf, my right hand would already be reaching for the next."[2] He also found a way to retrieve cereal boxes from a very high shelf by knocking them down with a pole and catching them before they hit the floor.

WORKING AT LA CONQUESTA

The story of the Yep family in America begins in 1915, when the family of Laurence's mother arrived from China. They settled first in Lima, Ohio, but soon moved to Clarksburg, West Virginia, where Laurence's maternal grandfather, Sing Thin Lee, bought a laundry business. Laurence's mother

Franche was born in Clarksburg, but the Lees moved to San Francisco when she was 10 years old.

In 1924, Laurence's father, then called Yep Gim Lew, arrived in the United States at the age of 10 and joined his father. Laurence's grandfather arrived years before and had taken a job as a houseboy in El Paso, Texas, but he found the desert climate disagreeable and soon moved to San Francisco. When he had saved enough money, he sent for his youngest son, who took the name of Thomas after he arrived in America. The Yeps could never afford the passage for Thomas's mother. She remained in China for the rest of her life, and she died there in the 1940s.

Thomas Yep's father found work as a houseboy in the home of a San Francisco pharmacist, Herbert Dugan. Houseboys performed any number of tasks for their employers, including cleaning, cooking, gardening, and chauffeuring. According to Yep, Dugan was a "big fat jolly bachelor with a broad face who liked to laugh."[3] Dugan regarded his Chinese houseboy as more than an employee. The two men were friends, and Dugan became particularly fond of Thomas. Dugan often took the boy on outings, which included many visits to the estate of a wealthy friend, Charmaine London, the widow of novelist Jack London. In later years, Dugan remained close to his houseboy and his son. Dugan and the Yeps parted ways during the Great Depression of the 1930s, when Dugan lost his pharmacy and could no longer afford a houseboy. Although he had little money, Dugan gave Thomas Yep one of his few valuable possessions: a pocket watch. Later, Thomas gave the watch to his son Laurence.

Franche Lee and Thomas Yep met as teenagers while they both attended Galileo High School in San Francisco.

Did you know...

Herbert Dugan, the San Francisco pharmacist who employed Laurence Yep's grandfather as a houseboy, lost his savings in the Great Depression. Dugan was very fond of his houseboy's son, and before parting ways with the Yeps, he gave young Thomas Yep a gold pocket watch.

Thomas Yep eventually gave the watch to his son Laurence. By then, the watch no longer worked, and years later, Yep decided to have it repaired. Although the repairman found that half of the watch's mechanism was missing when he opened the back of the watch, he was able to replace the parts and get the watch to work once again.

Since then, the fragile watch has broken many times, but Yep prizes it very much and he always gets it fixed. Yep said he keeps the watch in repair as a way to connect with the San Francisco of the past. This was the era shortly after the earthquake and fire that devastated San Francisco in 1906, when Herbert Dugan could afford to employ a Chinese houseboy. Said Yep, "The watch belongs to a San Francisco when horses still clopped on wide streets alongside the newer automobiles, and Victorian [homes] smelled of fresh wood and paint as San Francisco rebuilt itself."*

---

* Laurence Yep, "I Have a Watch," speech given at the University of California–Davis School of Education, January 19, 2005, p. 2.

By then, the Depression had hit America and most families struggled to pay the bills. Thomas Yep enrolled in college, but he had to drop out after a year to help his family earn money. Thomas found work as a fruit picker, and Franche Lee took a job as a housekeeper. They married and soon started a family. Tom was born in 1939 and Laurence followed in 1948. During World War II, Thomas Yep found a job as a welder in a shipyard. He saved his money and, when the war ended, he was able to buy the grocery store on Pierce Street.

The store had been named *La Conquesta*, a Spanish phrase that means "the conquest." Its previous owner was a Mexican-American man who was evidently proud of the Spanish conquistadors who conquered Mexico and South America, so he named his store after their deeds. Thomas Yep decided to keep the name because he had no money to buy a new sign.

The family grocery store would turn out to be the place where Yep gained valuable insight into people and their habits, which later helped him develop as a writer. He listened to their conversations, learned about their problems and how they faced the dilemmas in their lives, and learned what made them laugh and what made them sad. Although the Yeps lived in an African-American neighborhood, they also lived about two miles from San Francisco's Chinatown community. As a result, as Yep grew up, he heard many accents and ethnic expressions. He also saw how different people dressed, how they wore their hair, and the types of foods they preferred. Yep explained, "Working in our family store and getting to know our customers, I learned early on how to observe and listen to people. It was good training for a writer."[4]

ASTHMA ATTACKS

Yep did not want to become a writer when he was a young boy. Instead, he was fascinated by machines and aspired to be an engineer or a scientist, which pleased his father. Thomas shared his son's interest in science; he had been a chemistry major in college when he was forced to drop out. Recalled Yep,

> I thought of myself as a scientist. I was going to be a chemist. Like my father, I was fascinated by machines. My father wanted to know how machines worked, televisions, for instance. At one time, he filled our apartment with old TVs! On the other hand, he was always asking, "What if?" questions about machines. What if the world had a central energy source that broadcast power? There could be world peace because it would be possible to cut off the power to any nation that wanted to start a war.[5]

Like his father, Yep loved to tinker with small devices such as radios and clocks. In fact, Yep did not have much of an interest in books. Although he visited the library in his neighborhood occasionally, he rarely found much that interested him. On one visit, a librarian tried to interest him in the Homer Price series, which was written in the 1940s by author Robert McCloskey. The title character, Homer Price, lived in the small town of Centerburg, where he often found himself entangled in comical predicaments. His most famous adventure is *Homer Price and His Doughnut Machine*, which tells the story of a machine that continually makes doughnuts and cannot stop. Yep paged through the book and found little to interest him, because he knew no one who lived in a small town, rode a bicycle to school, or left the front door unlocked, as happened in the story.

Indeed, Yep did not have much of an interest in books until he began to suffer from asthma attacks. Asthma is a disease of the lungs that can make sufferers find it difficult to breathe. Today, asthma sufferers inhale a mist from a spray container that helps open their lungs. When Yep was a child in the 1950s and 1960s, however, there were few effective home remedies for asthma, and a doctor often had to come to the patient's home during attacks.

Yep's attacks were occasionally severe. Although Thomas and Franche were quick to summon the doctor, it was sometimes several hours before the physician could be tracked down. In the meantime, Yep was forced to sit up in bed and struggle to catch his breath; his mother and father often read to him while he waited for the doctor to come. During one of his attacks, his mother read *The Pirates in Oz* by Ruth Plumy Thompson, who based the book on the original stories about Oz written by L. Frank Baum. A short time later, after he recovered from the asthma attack, Yep hurried to the library, where he pored over the building's entire collection of Oz books. Once he exhausted the supply of Oz books in his neighborhood branch, Yep went to San Francisco's main library downtown, where he read all of the Oz books in that collection, as well.

The 40 books in the Oz series—the first of which is *The Wonderful Wizard of Oz*—tell the story of the magical kingdom of Oz, which is inhabited by witches, tiny elves known as Munchkins, winged monkeys, and other fantastic creatures like the Tin Woodman, Cowardly Lion, and Scarecrow. The Oz books enormously influenced Yep, who later wrote many books in the fantasy genre of fiction.

Yep also saw more in the Oz series than just stories about witches and magical spells. He was intrigued by the conflict in the stories, as the characters questioned each other's beliefs and faced difficult problems with no easy solutions. Even though these books were set in a magical make-believe land, to Yep the stories seemed a lot more real than the silly predicaments that Homer Price was forced to endure.

Once he read all the books in the Oz series, Yep searched for similar stories to read, and he soon discovered science fiction. In the 1950s, the science fiction books were easy to find on the library shelves because the publishers printed pictures of rocket ships on the spines (at the time, most science fiction stories for young readers featured rockets in the plots). He read every science fiction book in the local library, and he was particularly drawn to the work of novelist Alice Mary Norton, who wrote under the name Andre Norton. Although it was impossible to stargaze in his San Francisco neighborhood because bright city street lamps washed out the night sky, Norton's books introduced him to the science of astronomy. Yep found that Norton's stories sparked his imagination, as well:

> The real appeal of Norton's books was not the stars themselves but the exotic worlds she created with their mysterious, half-ruined cities. I already knew what it was like to see an area that had been abandoned. Half the fun of her books wasn't so much the plot or the characters but the universe itself she created. And through that sad, tragic landscape ran outlaws and outcasts with whom I could identify.[6]

JOURNALISM STUDENT

Yep may have been a dedicated fan of science fiction, but by the time he entered St. Ignatius High School, he still

After he finished with the Oz series, Yep found his way to the work of Andre Norton, who wrote books such as Here Abide Monsters *and the* Witch World *series. Norton, pictured above in 1999, died in 2005 after writing 300 novels.*

had more interest in science than in fiction. An excellent chemistry student who wanted to become a chemist, Yep enrolled in an English class in his senior year. His teacher challenged him to write a composition worthy of publication. Yep wrote a story and submitted it to a national magazine; when his story was rejected, he realized how much he wanted to see his work in print. Although he tried again and was rejected again, he persevered.

As Yep's class neared graduation, the priests who served as teachers at St. Ignatius took class members on a retreat into the countryside, where they encouraged the students to think about what they planned to do after high school. Yep believed he had already made up his mind to study chemistry in college and work as a chemist for the rest of his life. During the retreat, Yep went on long walks by himself and soon concluded that he did not want to spend the rest of his life locked in a laboratory. What he really wanted to do was write.

When Yep returned home to his family's apartment on Pierce Street, he broke the news to his parents. Although Thomas Yep had hoped his son would become a prosperous chemist and escape the long hours and hard work of the grocery store, he supported him. Yep's older brother Tom had graduated from college with a degree in physics; he had found a very lucrative job in the new business of manufacturing computers that had become very big in the nearby California city of San Jose. Still, Thomas Yep recognized his younger son's talent and burning ambition. In the fall of 1966, Yep enrolled as a journalism major at Marquette University in Milwaukee, Wisconsin.

Journalists are writers, but they do not write fiction. Instead, they write the news that appears in newspapers, magazines, television, or Internet news outlets. As a journalism student, Yep learned a lot about how to write news, but he was not happy. He missed San Francisco and his family, and as a native Californian he was unprepared for the cold Milwaukee winters. He constantly slipped on the icy sidewalks and streets. "No one told me about ice," he said. "Snow would fall. A thaw would partially melt it and then another spell of cold weather would freeze it. When more snow fell, it became a regular trap for a Californian. As I was shivering and continually falling, winter soon lost any appeal for me."[7]

Unfortunately, Yep was not very successful with journalism. In one class, his assignment was to write a story about the city's bus system. Yep shivered for an hour on a busy street corner as he gathered information about the buses that drove by. When he received his grade from the teacher, he was shocked to find that he had failed the assignment. It turned out that Yep had gotten many of the details about the buses incorrect. In news stories, inaccuracy is unacceptable. The teacher, impatient, told Yep that he had more talent for fiction than fact. The comment was not meant to encourage Yep to start to write fiction, but to persuade him that he had no future as a news reporter.

Yep also felt like an outsider at Marquette. Indeed, few Asians made their homes in Milwaukee. In San Francisco, Yep had been one among the thousands of people of Asian ancestry who lived in the city. To escape from his troubles at college, Yep sat behind his typewriter and wrote short stories. While at Marquette, he made a good friend, Joanne Ryder, who was editor of the school literary magazine, the *Marquette Journal*. Ryder encouraged him to write fiction and also introduced him to several children's stories, including *Alice in Wonderland*; *The Lion, the Witch and the Wardrobe;* and other books in the Narnia series, as well as *Winnie the Pooh*.

In fact, Yep became a very active member on the staff of the *Marquette Journal*. He wrote short stories for the publication, helped secure the art and photographs that illustrated the stories, and wrote poetry. Yep also helped paint Joanne Ryder's office. A romance soon developed between Yep and Ryder, and the coupled married after they finished college.

At first, Yep's short stories were inspired by the urban Milwaukee neighborhood where he lived. He wrote contemporary and dramatic stories that he later admitted to himself were not very good. The professional fiction magazines agreed, and they sent him short letters of rejection. Finally, he decided to write science fiction stories. He said,

> It seems so obvious that I should have been trying science fiction from the very beginning. I liked the genre and I also like science; but part of the writing process is finding the best way to express yourself as a writer. The Irish writer, George Bernard Shaw, wrote several mediocre novels until he finally decided to try plays and became famous for writing those. His most famous play, *Pygmalion*, eventually became the Broadway and movie hit *My Fair Lady*.
>
> In any event, I sat down and began to write a story about a time when San Francisco had fallen into the sea during an earthquake. The hero of the story goes back to the ruins to try to discover his roots. He thinks he's a human but discovers that he's an alien.[8]

Yep titled the story "The Selchey Kids." In 1968, the story was accepted for publication in *If*, a national science fiction and fantasy magazine. When the story was published, the magazine's editor, Frederik Pohl, wrote a note that was printed alongside the story. The editor's note said, "A young San Franciscan who is now a sophomore in college, nineteen-year-old Laurence Yep is clearly headed for great things!"[9] A year later, "The Selchey Kids" was included in the anthology *The World's Best Science Fiction*. With his first published story, Yep was able to establish himself as one of the country's leading voices in science fiction and fantasy writing.

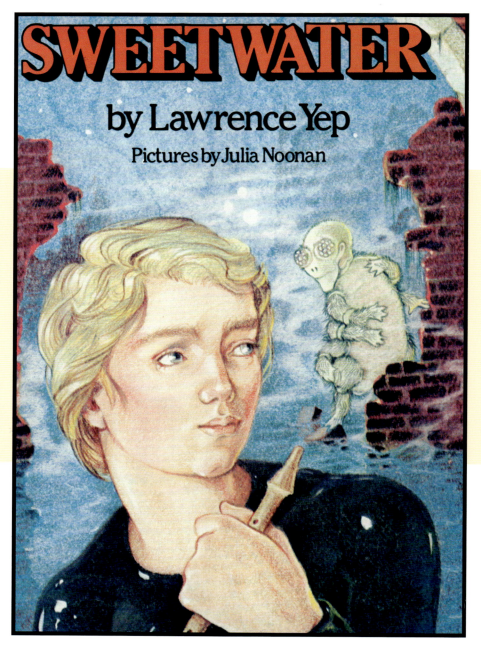

SWEETWATER

by Lawrence Yep

Pictures by Julia Noonan

Yep's first novel, Sweetwater, tells the story of Tyree, a young man who must overcome a hostile environment to survive on the planet Harmony. Yep had found success writing science fiction short stories, so he decided to stick with the genre in writing his debut novel.

3

Bridge Between Two Cultures

WHEN LAURENCE YEP lived in Milwaukee, he once walked into a Chinese restaurant to eat dinner. Soon, the two owners approached him and started to speak in Chinese. When Yep explained that he could not speak Chinese, the two men turned away and left him alone for the rest of his meal.

Over the years, Yep has had many similar encounters. Since he did not speak Chinese and had little understanding of Chinese culture, old-world Chinese immigrants such as the Milwaukee restaurant owners would not accept him. At home, Thomas and Franche Yep spoke English and encouraged their boys to become fully Americanized.

In addition, the Yep family observed Catholicism, rather than the traditional Chinese religions of Taoism and Buddhism.

As a boy of Asian descent, Yep occasionally experienced prejudice and racism from people of other cultures, too. Although his father was once attacked and beaten up by a group of white boys, Yep did not face this type of bigotry. Still, as one of the few Asian children in an African-American community, Yep regarded himself an outsider in his own neighborhood. Indeed, he recalled that Asians faced a lot of discrimination in the 1950s. After all, the memories of World War II and the fight against the Japanese were still fresh in the minds of Americans. Later, Americans fought against Korean and Chinese communists in the Korean War, which further enforced people's misconceptions about Asians. The prejudice even spilled over into the games Yep and his friends played as boys. Yep recalled, "I was the all-purpose Asian. When (my friends and I) played war, I was the Japanese who got killed; then, when the Korean war came along, I was a North Korean communist."[1]

SWEETWATER

At Marquette, Yep eventually gave up journalism and changed his major to English. His goal was to obtain an advanced degree and teach English at a college; he also planned to write fiction. After he finished his sophomore year at Marquette, he transferred to the University of California–Santa Cruz, which was close to his family's home in San Francisco. After graduating in 1970, Yep began to teach English at the State University of New York in Buffalo. At the same time, Yep took his own advanced English courses, and he wrote his first novel. Since he had found success as a writer of science fiction stories, Yep decided to stay within that genre. Published in 1973, *Sweetwater* tells the story of Tyree, a young man who must overcome a hostile environment to survive on the planet Harmony.

Sweetwater describes three communities: the Silkies, the Mainlanders, and the Argans. According to the story, Earth has been depleted of its natural resources and must send missions to other planets to obtain food, ore, minerals, and other materials for the mother planet. Ancestors of the Silkies and Mainlanders took part in one such voyage, but their starship broke down after they arrived on the planet Harmony, and they were forced to stay. The two communities separated and became suspicious and hostile toward one another. The Silkies, of which Tyree is a member, were once the servants of the Mainlanders, who consider themselves superior to the Silkies. The Argans, the native inhabitants on the planet, are hostile to both the Silkies and the Mainlanders.

To complicate matters, Harmony's cities have been flooded by seawater, which forces the inhabitants of the planet to adapt to a new environment. The Silkies have elected to stay in the flooded coastal cities, where they struggle to survive, but the Mainlanders have retreated inland. The name of the book refers to the ability of the Silkies to find fresh, drinkable water—"sweetwater"—beneath the surface of the planet.

Certainly, *Sweetwater* is a work of science fiction that takes the reader into many fantastic places and journeys through space, as well as encounters with strange life forms. *Sweetwater* is also a story about Laurence Yep. His own life served as inspiration for the story of Tyree, an outsider on his own planet who tries to understand the culture of the Argans and learn their ways. As a Chinese American,

Yep also felt like an outsider. First, he was a Chinese boy who grew up in an African-American neighborhood in San Francisco, and then he was a lonely college student in Milwaukee who could not quite find a place to fit in.

Yep also regarded himself as an outsider in American culture: He was not quite American and not quite Chinese. In other words, he found that he lived on the border of two cultures. Tyree struggles to adapt to a different culture on Harmony just as Yep, as a Chinese American, struggled to adapt to white society in America. Said Yep, "In writing about alienated people and aliens in my science fiction, I was writing about myself as a Chinese American."[2]

OLD-COUNTRY CUSTOMS

After the publication of *Sweetwater*, Yep wrote *Dragonwings*. In his second book, Yep departed from science fiction and began to explore how Chinese immigrants found ways to adapt to life in America.

Yep did not abandon this theme after *Dragonwings* was published in 1975. As a novelist, Yep would often chronicle the lives of Chinese characters who must deal with old-country customs, language barriers, racism, and other issues as they make their homes in America. "As a child, I hated Chinese school. I wanted to be as American as possible," Yep said. "Then, in my early twenties, I became very interested in my Chinese roots."[3] Indeed, Yep said, he felt a responsibility to serve "as a bridge between two cultures."[4]

As Yep wrote about ordinary Chinese immigrants who lived in American society, he realized he had to repair decades of prejudice perpetuated by the authors of novels and screenplays. For years, Asian characters seldom held significant roles in American literature or in the movies. Usually, they were included in books as houseboys, gardeners, or occasionally as sidekicks, such as Kato, the Japanese chauffeur for the American crime buster Green Hornet.

Even when Asians were used as major characters, they were often stereotyped as comic figures or evil villains. Among the most famous Asians in literature were Charlie Chan, the Honolulu detective forced to suffer the blunders and awkwardness of his overeager "number one son," and Dr. Fu Manchu, the Chinese madman intent on world conquest. Yep introduced a different type of Asian-American character, an outsider who did not quite fit into society, yet who possessed courage, intelligence, and a moral compass. Said Yep,

> It has been my aim to counter various stereotypes as presented in the media. Dr. Fu Manchu and his yellow hordes, Charlie Chan and his fortune-cookie wisdom, the laundryman and cooks of the movie and television Westerns, and the houseboys of various comedies present an image of Chinese not as they really are but as they exist in the mind of White America. I wanted to show that Chinese Americans are human beings upon whom America has had a unique effect.[5]

After the publication of *Dragonwings*, Yep and Ryder left Buffalo and returned to California, where they established a home in Pacific Grove, a community on the coast about 75 miles south of San Francisco. Meanwhile, Yep began to teach English at San Jose City College.

Yep's next two books were contemporary stories that further explore the roots of Chinese-American society.

Yep often recounts the lives of Chinese characters who must deal with old-country customs, language barriers, racism, and other issues as they make their homes in America. The picture above, taken in 1921, shows a Chinese man smoking a long pipe in San Francisco's Chinatown.

Child of the Owl was published in 1977, and *Sea Glass* was published in 1979. In *Child of the Owl*, a Chinese girl who grows up in an American community learns about her heritage from her grandmother. The book is set in San Francisco's Chinatown in the 1960s.

SEEKING ACCEPTANCE

In the story, Casey's mother has died. Her father, Barney, is a gambler who takes her from town to town as he makes bets on horses. When Barney is hospitalized, Casey moves to Chinatown to live with her grandmother's family. As her grandmother, Paw-Paw, holds onto the old-world customs of Chinese society, the younger members of the family continue to become Americanized. For example, Casey's cousin is a college student and president of a sorority. Casey is clearly uneasy in her new home; she does not like the company of other Chinese people and wishes she could live among white people again. She is reluctant to eat with chopsticks and to drink tea instead of soda, although she finds that she enjoys the tea just as much.

To help Casey understand how the Chinese who live in America must hold onto their roots, Paw-Paw tells her the story of an owl named Jasmine who becomes human. Jasmine marries a human and raises a family, but in her soul she remains an owl. Casey finds comfort in the story of the owl, and she realizes that it is okay to feel American on the outside and Chinese on the inside. Casey says, "I realized that you don't have to believe in the stories. You don't even have to believe in the gods they're about; but you ought to know those stories and the gods and also know your ancestors once believed in them and tried to model their lives after certain good spirits."[6]

Did you know...

Chinese is actually a group of languages, not one language on its own. The most widely spoken language in the Chinese family is Mandarin, though people who live in different parts of the country might speak Wu, Min, or Cantonese.

As a boy, Laurence Yep's family spoke English at home, so Yep never learned Chinese. Although he did not live in San Francisco's Chinatown, a large number of Chinese-American students attended his Catholic elementary school. When Yep was in the fourth grade, the nuns who taught at his school decided to try to teach Chinese to the students. Yep was a most reluctant student. In his autobiography, *The Lost Garden*, Yep wrote, "I was placed in the dummies' class where simple Chinese words were taught with even simpler ones. However, we spoke no Chinese at home so I didn't even know the teacher's basic commands. As a result, I had to watch the other students and take out a book when they did or put it away."*

Yep said he resented the nuns' efforts to teach him Chinese. He decided to memorize the Chinese alphabet and the Chinese words rather than learn what the letters or words meant. At the end of the class, Yep received a passing grade, but he learned virtually no Chinese.

* Laurence Yep, *The Lost Garden*. Englewood Cliffs, N.Y: Julian Messner, 1991, p. 52.

Yep's next book, *Sea Glass*, further explored the theme of a young person of Chinese ancestry who seeks acceptance in American society. Unlike Casey, who learns to accept her Chinese roots after she moves to Chinatown, Craig Chin finds himself rejected by white Americans as he moves out of Chinatown and into a small town named Concepcion, where Asian faces are not common sights. Unlike Casey, Craig does speak Chinese, but that only serves to alienate him from the white children in town, who call him "Buddha Man." When Craig tries to be more like the whites, his uncle reprimands him for his neglect of his Chinese roots. Frustrated, Craig says, "If the kids thought of me as a foreigner, the old Chinese here thought of me as an American."[7] Craig is another character who lives along a border; he is not quite American and not quite Chinese. As he did in *Sweetwater*, Yep drew from his own experience of being caught between two cultures to craft the character of Craig Chin.

The Star Fisher, published in 1991, explores the experience of Chinese immigrants who put down roots in a most unlikely place: the mountains of West Virginia. Yep sets the story in the small town of Clarksburg, the same town where his mother's parents opened a laundry nearly a century ago. Yep sets the story in 1927, at a time when his mother, Franche, was a teenager. The main character of *The Star Fisher*, 15-year-old Joan Lee, is based on his mother. Like Yep's mother and her family, Joan and her parents have come to Clarksburg to open a laundry.

When the Lees arrive, everyone in town assumes they have migrated to Clarksburg from China, but that is not true. Like Yep's mother's family, Joan and her parents are from Ohio. Indeed, residents of Clarksburg are truly surprised that the Lees speak English.

The Lees meet a lot of kind people in West Virginia, but there is also a veil of prejudice and racism that hangs over the town. Some of the townspeople make fun of the Lees and they use the derogatory term "chink" when they refer to people of Chinese ancestry. With courage, the Lees endure the taunts.

Unlike Casey, Joan is proud of her heritage and makes no attempt to hide it. Joan is also unlike Craig because she does not need to battle for acceptance among other Chinese people. Slowly, Joan wins the acceptance of some of the whites in Clarksburg. She makes friends with adults and teens, learns how to fit into white society as she holds onto her Chinese roots, and helps her parents assimilate into the Clarksburg community.

According to Yep, the story of his mother's family in Clarksburg is not unique. He explained that after they emigrated from China, many Chinese families preferred not to live in the Chinatowns of big cities. Instead, they fanned out across America and settled in places like Clarksburg. He said,

> Chinese families refused to be confined to the Chinatowns on the two coasts and were searching for a place in America for themselves back in the 1920s and earlier. I have met Chinese Americans who were born and raised in rural towns in such states as Arkansas, Mississippi, and Oklahoma. In this sense, *The Star Fisher* is as much their story as it is my family's.[8]

As Yep continued to explore the story of the Chinese in America, his focus shifted from his own experiences, as well as from the obstacles that his ancestors were forced to face and overcome. Indeed, China is a country with a long and colorful history, and Yep soon found plenty to write about as he drew stories from the land of his ancestors.

Yep writes about a wide variety of subjects in his historical fiction. One such topic is the building of the transcontinental railroad, in which many Chinese immigrants participated. Above, the camp site of the Chinese crew is shown beside a construction train in Nevada.

4

Telling Stories From History

AFTER THE PUBLICATION of *Child of the Owl* and *Sea Glass*, Laurence Yep was eager to return to historical fiction. Both critics and his readers had praised his second novel, *Dragonwings*, and Yep felt that there were many more stories to tell about true events in the history of the Chinese people and their paths to America. Soon, he came across the story of the Taiping Rebellion in China. Yep thought the rebellion could serve as the backdrop for a story he would weave around a young girl's will to survive.

Fought between 1851 and 1864, the Taiping Rebellion is regarded as one of history's bloodiest civil wars; historians believe that at least 20 million Chinese were killed. The rebels were loyal to Chinese Christian leader Hong Xiu-quan, who sought to overthrow the corrupt Qing dynasty of emperors. The rebellion is named after Hong's movement, *Taiping Tianguo*, which in English means "Heavenly King-dom of Peace."

Yep's book about the rebellion is titled *The Serpent's Children*, and it tells about a girl named Cassia Young whose family joins the rebellion. Cassia's story commences in 1849, just as the uprising begins. By the end of the book, the rebellion is doomed, and her family looks toward the "Golden Mountain" for a new beginning.

The Golden Mountain is the name that many Chinese in the nineteenth century gave to America. Doomed to endure poverty, famine, civil war, and life under regimes of cor-rupt dictators, it was the dream of many Chinese people to sail across the ocean, where they would find the Golden Mountain in California. Published in 1984, *The Serpent's Children* would become the first in what Yep expects will be a nine-volume collection of books known as the Golden Mountain Chronicles, which follows Cassia's family, the Youngs, as they endure strife in China and then escape across the ocean.

Certainly, the story of the Youngs closely parallels the story of the Yeps in America, and that is why Yep included *Dragonwings* in the series. In addition, he considers *Child of the Owl* and *Sea Glass* among the books in the series, as well. Although not truly historical novels, *Child of the Owl* and *Sea Glass* nevertheless provide important chapters in the development of the Chinese-American experience.

Other books in the Golden Mountain Chronicles include *Mountain Light*, a sequel to *The Serpent's Children* set in

Did you know...

Most of Laurence Yep's stories are written from the point of view of the main character. He writes in what is known as the first person, in which the main character refers to himself or herself as "I."

Yep said he prefers to write in that style because he envisions himself as the narrator; therefore, he feels as though he is part of the story. "I like the lens that it provides," he said. "It makes me focus on my own experience in a certain way when I write in the first person."*

An author may also write in the second person or the third person. One who writes in the second person tells the story from the point of view of the reader; however, in the text the reader is referred to as "you." This technique is rarely used in fiction.

Much more common, though, are books written in the third person. Authors who write in the third person tell the story from the point of view of an outside observer. Characters in the book are referred to as "he" or "she" or by their names.

---

* Quoted in "Laurence Yep's Interview Transcript," Scholastic Inc., http://books. scholastic.com/teachers/authorsandbooks/ authorstudies/authorhome.jsp?authorID=10 1&displayName=Interview%20Transcript.

1885; *Dragon's Gate*, which relates the story of Cassia's 14-year-old adopted son, Otter, who immigrates to America in 1867 and finds work as one of the Chinese laborers who built the transcontinental railroad; and *The Traitor*, which relates the story of the 1885 miners' riot in Rock Springs, Wyoming, in which hapless Chinese laborers were murdered by a rampaging mob. Otter is also the featured character in *The Traitor*; after he finishes his work on the railroad, Otter makes his way to Wyoming, where he finds work at the Rock Springs mine.

Another book in the series is titled *Thief of Hearts*, a sequel to *Child of the Owl*. Set in 1995, Casey Young's daughter, Stacy, and her great-grandmother must defend a Chinese immigrant girl accused of theft. Overall, the books of the Golden Mountain Chronicles recount some 150 years of history of the Young family in China and America.

TREASURE HUNT

Writers of historical fiction take real events and use them as backdrops for their fictional stories. The actual plot of the story may have very little to do with the historical event that is depicted in the book; nevertheless, the characters are part of the story, and their lives will become entangled with the activities of the real-life players in the drama. Indeed, some authors use real characters when they write historical fiction: Presidents, famous military leaders, statesmen, patriots, rebels, and other figures from history are routinely part of stories concocted by fiction writers. In fact, writers make up dialogue and put their words in the mouths of real people. In the genre of historical fiction, this technique is acceptable.

Sir Walter Scott, shown above, is considered the first great historical novelist. He wrote tales of adventure and intrigue, such as Ivanhoe *and* Rob Roy, *which took place in England and Scotland.*

Early nineteenth-century Scottish author Sir Walter Scott is regarded as the first great historical novelist. *Ivanhoe* and *Rob Roy*, his stories of adventure and intrigue in England and Scotland, are considered classics. In America, nineteenth-century author James Fenimore Cooper's books about colonial times, such as the classic *The Last of the Mohicans*, are thought to be as historically accurate as any nonfiction book written about the era. Another important example of historical fiction in America is *The Red Badge of Courage*, a novel about the Civil War written in 1895 by Stephen Crane. Although Crane did not fight in the Civil War and never named a battle in the book, his description of what historians suggest is the Battle of Chancellorsville is as accurate as any eyewitness account.

A much more recent example of American historical fiction is *The Killer Angels*, written in 1974 by Michael Shaara. The book tells the story of the Battle of Gettysburg during the Civil War. Shaara wrote about the real officers and soldiers who fought in the battle, but he made up the dialogue and placed his own words in the mouths of such characters as Robert E. Lee, James Longstreet, and Joshua Lawrence Chamberlain.

Historical fiction has long been a part of literature in America, as well as in Europe. Writers who specialize in historical fiction will research their subject matter as carefully as a historian might research the same subject for a nonfiction book. Typically, Yep researches a topic for months before he writes the first word of his manuscript. In fact, Yep said it took years of historical research into the Rock Springs riot before he was prepared to write *The Traitor*. Yep explained, "Historical research has always seemed like a treasure hunt to me: in dusty libraries I find information I can use to give voice to the ghosts from the past."[1]

MISSING FROM AMERICAN FICTION

According to Yep, what has been largely missing from American historical fiction is the story of the Chinese immigrants and their role in building the country. "The history books of the '50s—you would think America was founded by all white, Anglo-Saxon males," he said.[2]

Dragon's Gate is Yep's response to that kind of bias. The role of the transcontinental railroad in the development of the United States as a nation cannot be understated. Before the railroad connected the eastern half of the country with the Pacific Coast, there were few ways for settlers and others to make their way to California. Wagon trains were slow, cumbersome, and expensive. Pioneer families who traveled alone risked starvation, freezing weather, and other hostile conditions. As for communication with the West Coast, easterners had to depend on the Pony Express or a network of telegraph lines that were largely unreliable. Completed in 1869, the railroad linked hundreds of miles of track. Some had been laid west by Irish laborers in the employ of the Union Pacific Railroad, and some had been laid east by Chinese workers in the employ of the Central Pacific Railroad. On May 10, 1869, the two railroads were connected at Promontory Summit, Utah.

At first, officials of the Central Pacific had their doubts about the Chinese laborers because they thought they were too small and frail to perform such heavy work. Nevertheless, the Chinese turned out to be hard workers, and soon the Central Pacific was willing to hire any Chinese man who could swing a pick or wield a shovel. Thousands of Chinese men responded to the call, and they left their jobs as houseboys or kitchen or laundry workers for dangerous jobs that paid no more than pennies a day. Many of the workers were immigrants right off the boat from China, who were scooped up by railroad bosses in constant need of men to work on the railroad.

Although the Chinese laborers played such an important role in the creation of the most important link between the eastern and western sections of the United States, Yep found little of substance when he looked for their story in the history books. He said,

> If the history books mentioned them at all, it was usually in the chapter on the building of the transcontinental railroad; and even then, it is usually only a sentence; and yet their achievements deserved far more, for they performed heroic labors—even dangling from baskets down the faces of sheer cliffs to drive holes into the hard granite with chisels and hammers and then packing the holes with gunpowder (and hoping that they could be pulled up in time once they lit the fuse).
>
> Moreover, these were men and boys who came from a Chinese climate in the same latitude as tropical Mexico, and they were brought straight into the Sierras during the worst blizzard of the [nineteenth] century so that at times they had to live underneath the snow.[3]

Hundreds of Chinese men died on the route. After the last spike was driven at Promontory Summit, the Central Pacific Railroad shipped back 10 tons of bones to be buried in China. It is estimated that the bones represented some 1,200 laborers, or 10 percent of the workforce, who died while doing their jobs. A significant chapter in the story of the railroad involved a strike called by the Chinese workers, who demanded higher wages. They also felt abused by their bosses and wanted better treatment. Yep has made the strike an important part of the plot of *Dragon's Gate*.

Dragon's Gate, which was published in 1993, tells the story of Cassia's adopted son, Otter, as he leaves a region of southern China known as the Middle Kingdom and arrives in San Francisco in 1867. Otter soon joins a work crew and heads high into the Sierra Mountains to dig a tunnel and lay track for the railroad, where he must haul rock and rubble away from the work site. In China, Otter's family was wealthy and influential, but when he arrives in America he learns that all Chinese are equals. His Uncle Foxfire, whom he sees in the Chinese work camp, tells Otter, "Get it through your head, boy, or you won't live out a day. In the Middle Kingdom, you and I were on the top of the heap, but here we're on the bottom. Question the bosses or talk back, and they'll kill you in a dozen different ways."[4]

Otter survives the ordeal and is even on hand at Promontory Summit when the final, golden spike is driven into the ground. As a Chinese laborer, however, he is not allowed to attend the ceremony. In fact, Otter guesses that the final spike has been hammered into the ground because he can hear white men cheering in the distance. "They can have their little ceremony," he tells the other laborers. "We know the truth."[5] Still, the book ends with a note of optimism, as Otter looks forward to the rest of his life in America.

Yep has found that his young readers can relate to his historical fiction. They are able to put themselves in the place of his characters and draw comparisons in their own lives with the adventures and challenges Yep describes in his books. He said, "I know children of all ages identify with Otter's dilemma: he is the helpless victim of a world created by adults. Though the risk is far greater and the humor far less, Otter is as [much] the prey of adults' apparently arbitrary rules as Alice is when she enters Wonderland."[6]

LESSONS FROM HISTORY

In addition to the Golden Mountain Chronicles, Yep has used his books to explore other significant moments in history. For one book, *Hiroshima: A Novella*, Yep took a step away from Chinese and Chinese-American history and delved into one of the darkest chapters in the history of Japan: the atomic bomb strikes on the cities of Hiroshima and Nagasaki that ended World War II.

Yep's book tells of the devastation of the Japanese city of Hiroshima. The story focuses on a young Japanese girl, Sachi, who survived the bombing but was disfigured by the flash of fire and fallout. Later, Sachi will be one of the "Hiroshima Maidens," Japanese girls who received reconstructive surgery in the United States. In the book, Yep describes the bomb blast:

> There is a terrible wind. Houses collapse like boxes. Windows break everywhere. Broken glass swirls like angry insects.
>
> The wind strikes Sachi back like a hammer and picks her up. She feels as if she has fallen into boiling oil. It tears away her special hood and even her clothes. The wind sweeps her into the whirlwind of glass.
>
> There is no time to scream. There is no one to hear.
>
> There is only darkness. . . .
>
> And Sachi mercifully passes out.[7]

As with the Chinese railroad laborers and the victims of the Rock Springs riots, Yep thought that the story of the Hiroshima Maidens had been largely ignored by the history book, and explained, "Sachi is a composite of several children who were in Hiroshima when the bomb dropped and who later came to the United States. We should all draw lessons from their suffering and their courage."[8]

Yep, shown above, says he spends no less than six months doing research for each of his novels. The research and preparation he does for each book shows in the richness of detail he is able to impart through his writing.

5

A Writer's View of the World

WHETHER LAURENCE YEP writes historical fiction like *Hiroshima: A Novella* or *Dragon's Gate*, or science fiction stories like *Sweetwater*, he thoroughly researches the topics for his stories. In fact, Yep said he spends no less than six months in research on a book and sometimes much longer. For *Dragon's Gate*, Yep studied the stories behind the construction of the transcontinental railroad for 20 years before he felt qualified to write his own story.

That does not mean that for 20 years Yep researched only the story of the transcontinental railroad and did nothing else.

Actually, over that period of years he would go back to the project from time to time. For example, while on a trip to another city, if he had the opportunity, he visited the local library to see if there was anything on file about the railroad that he had not seen elsewhere. Frequently, he found some good information. "Sometimes, research is like building a house out of toothpicks," Yep said. "But before you can build that house, you have to find the toothpicks scattered all over a country. So wherever I go, I check out the library."[1] In fact, while he researched the story, he read one account published in a Sacramento, California, newspaper that stated that the Chinese railroad workers had gone on strike partially because their bosses had whipped them or would not allow them to quit their jobs. That is the type of obscure yet significant detail that can add a lot of color to a writer's manuscript.

It is important for Yep and other writers to become experts on the subjects of their stories so that the readers will accept the stories as realistic. In other words, good research helps make the stories believable. Writers may look through dozens of resources to prepare themselves. To write *Hiroshima: A Novella*, Yep drew on more than 20 resources to reconstruct his story of the bombing. For *Dragon's Gate*, Yep read 16 books about the railroad and also consulted dozens of old newspaper stories published in San Francisco and other California cities, which included Sacramento and Stockton. Finally, he traveled the route of the original railroad and trekked over the terrain in the Sierra Mountains where the Chinese laborers laid the tracks and dug the tunnels. While he researches his books, Yep may read additional books on the subject, and he may also look through old newspapers, magazines, and similar sources. The Internet has helped many writers find material that has been made available online by libraries, universities, and other institutions. Yep makes use of such resources, to be sure, but he also searches through original documents, even old maps and photographs that may be on file in the back rooms of libraries and historical societies. Original documents and photographs, Yep believes, help his readers know what it is like to live in the time period and the place he has chosen to write about. An old photograph, for example, includes many tiny details that Yep can use to explain what it was like in the world of his characters. He said,

> From sources such as these, I've learned, for instance, that in San Francisco's Chinatown in the late 1800s there were three shooting galleries and some lumberyards. If you were walking through the streets in those days, you might have heard the pop pop pop of shooting galleries going off and the sound of hand-powered saws. I put background noises such as these into my stories because they make for more vivid writing. By now, having done so much research, when I go for a walk in Chinatown I can "see" all the long-gone buildings that lined the streets at different times in the past.[2]

SCAFFOLDING OF A SHIP

Yep also constantly writes little notes about things he sees or hears, or memories he may have. In fact, when he wrote *Dragonwings,* he went back to hundreds of notes he had scribbled over the years about what he had learned about his own family. He keeps all those notes because he knows that at some point in the future, they may help him craft a story.

According to Yep, ideas for books come from many sources. Of course, since he has written many historical stories about Chinese Americans, true historical events

Did you know...

Readers of Laurence Yep's novels have come across some characters with unusual names. For example, *Dragon's Gate* included characters named "Doggie," "Packy," and "Otter." *Dragonwings* featured a character named "Hand Clap" and another named "Lefty." Other characters in Yep's books have been named "Squeaky," "Runt," and "Curly."

Where does Yep find such colorful names for his characters?

"The names come from various sources," he said. "Some of them are nicknames I heard in Chinatown because the Chinese Americans from a certain generation had colorful nicknames like Doggie. Sometimes I like the sound of a name, or sometimes there's a hidden meaning."*

In *Dragonwings*, he wanted a character to symbolize the authority, or law, of the white people of San Francisco, so he named her "Miss Whitelaw." For other characters, Yep simply draws names from his memories of real people. In one book, Yep named a character "Purdy" because he once had an English teacher by that name.

* Quoted in "Laurence Yep's Interview Transcript," Scholastic Inc., http://books.scholastic.com/teachers/authorsandbooks/authorstudies/authorhome.jsp?authorID=101&displayName=Interview%20Transcript.

such as the construction of the transcontinental railroad and the Rock Springs riots have provided backdrops for his tales. Yep believes, however, that ideas can also come from tiny and unusual sources. He said, "Good writing brings out what's special in ordinary things. . . . I actually wrote a book about the time I gave my brother a pet alligator. But really, writing only requires taking a step to the side and looking at something from a slightly different angle. So you can find unicorns in the garden, and monsters sitting next to you."[3]

Sometimes, the story simply stems from an image that grows in Yep's head. For example, Yep conceived the plot for *Dragonwings* after he imagined an airplane soaring over a hill. He soon started to weave a story around the image, placing a character like his father at the controls of the plane. In fact, when he sat down to write *Dragonwings*, he wrote the last chapter first. That was the chapter that described Windrider's flight over the California hills. After he finished the last chapter, he wrote the rest of the book.

According to Yep, writers must train themselves to look at the world differently from other people. When Yep worked as a college professor and taught a writing course, he would tell students to take any object in a room, such as a light bulb, and try to imagine the light bulb as a living creature. How would the light bulb talk to other light bulbs? How would the light bulb eat or find its food? What type of world would it be if all the creatures were light bulbs? When the writer has gone through that exercise and has come up with ideas about how light bulbs would communicate or find nourishment, the next step is for the writer to make up a story about light bulbs. The story may be humorous or rather dramatic. In other words, Yep said, writers must constantly use their imaginations and come up with fresh ideas about how to tell stories.

Many writers seem to think they need to go to exotic locations or actually experience exciting situations in order to write about them, but that is not necessarily true. Yep believes that as long as writers have fertile imaginations, and they have spent an adequate amount of time in the library, they should be able to tell the story. He said,

> Children or college students seem to think they have to go to Paris, or they have to have a shipwreck before they can begin writing. And the fact is that's not true. I would actually have exercises in writing, where I would have the students write about their desktop; because there are different things you can do, different tricks you can use to really focus in on what you're looking at. And because, really, all it requires is looking at an object and then taking one step to the side and looking at that object from a slightly different angle.[4]

Like most writers, Yep drafts an outline before he starts writing. The outline lays out ideas for the characters and the chapters and describes how the plot will unfold. He does not stick rigidly to the outline, however, and will let the book head off into a different direction. "It's like the scaffolding around a ship," he said. "Sometimes halfway through a battleship, I realize I should be making an aircraft carrier, and so I have to change the scaffolding."[5]

SEVEN DRAFTS

Once the research is finished and the outline has been prepared, it is time to write the story. Before he begins work each day, Yep follows a ritual. First, he tries to write at the same time every day. Yep finds that he is better able to prepare himself mentally for the workday ahead if he knows exactly what time of day he will be required to think about his story. He also tries to work the same amount of time every day. Typically, Yep spends about four hours a day at his keyboard.

To write, Yep goes into his home office and shuts the door. Then, he closes his eyes and practices breathing exercises. When he closes his eyes, he finds that it helps him clear his mind of other thoughts and concentrate solely on the story he intends to write. Yep explained, "When I finally open my eyes, I get a flood of information and feel I've reconnected myself with the world and am ready to begin."[6]

Yep makes many revisions to his manuscripts. His 1982 novel *Dragon of the Lost Sea* was rewritten seven times. In fact, the book originally focused on two young suburban boys who find themselves in the midst of an adventure based on Chinese mythology. Yep introduced two minor characters: a dragon and her "pet" boy. As he worked on the book, Yep realized that the two minor characters were much more fascinating than the two original main characters. He tossed out the manuscript and the original outline, and this time he made the dragon and the boy the central characters in the plot. According to Yep, the dragon and the boy "became such vivid characters for me that I finally realized that the story had to be about them."[7]

Writer's block can be a problem for many writers. Typically, a writer crafts a story and produces dozens or even hundreds of pages and then, suddenly, the writer runs into a creative wall. He or she may have gotten the story's characters into a dangerous situation and does not know how to get them out of it. Perhaps one of the characters has been planned poorly and does not add much to the story. The story may simply not be as exciting as the writer had hoped. Obviously, the book needs a revision, but the writer is just unable to come up with the solution. Yep said he has often been a victim of writer's block. His solution is to simply put the story aside for a time and work on something else. After taking a few days or weeks off from the story, Yep finds he can return to the problem with a fresh eye.

MAKING MEMORIES COME TO LIFE

There is no question that Laurence Yep is a very successful novelist. He has written more than 60 books, and he earns a good living by writing. Still, as he looks back on his career, Yep has decided he does not write for the money. In fact, when he sold his first story, "The Selchey Kids," to *If* magazine, the publication paid him the very modest fee of a penny per word. In other words, he earned only a few dollars for the story, which is hardly the type of payday that would suggest that a fiction writer could have a lucrative career. Yep said, "I never really expected to make a living as a writer."[8]

In fact, when Yep encounters young people with an interest in a career as a writer, he urges them not to write for the money, but for personal satisfaction and to see his or her work in print. He also urges young writers to accept rejection. Yep sent stories to many publications that turned him down before he finally found a magazine that was willing to publish "The Selchey Kids." "Writers are writers and they love to write," he said. "But we don't always publish what we write."[9]

Yep also urges writers not to be discouraged if their work is rejected, even if takes years to find a publisher who will accept their stories. When he started to write stories in high school, he knew many other young people who also aspired to be writers. Over the years, they lost their enthusiasm and gave up; according to Yep, a writer must be persistent. When young writers come to him for advice on how to write, Yep tells them,

> The first thing is to write about what they know. And the second thing is to try to use all their senses when they write. Too many writers just use their eyes. It's more striking if you can use smells, for instance. Try and map your world by smells. Beyond that, you just have to pay attention to the world around you—gestures that a person makes, how they change their voice. I've taught creative writing . . . and it's surprising how much detail people leave out. Once you connect these details to your memories, you can start making them come to life.[10]

In Chinese culture, dragons are thought to have many powers and are regarded as friendly and helpful to humans. In order to write about dragons in his books, Yep had to decide how they would be characterized. One thing he decided to do was to base the way dragons fly on gliders, which are aircraft without engines, like the one shown above.

6

Dragons, Imps, and Aliens

IN CHINESE CULTURE, dragons are believed to have held many powers, particularly the power to bring rain. As a result, farmers worshipped dragons because they needed rain to make their crops grow. Chinese emperors also thought that dragons brought them power, so they designed their thrones to resemble dragons and wore clothing decorated with images of dragons.

In ancient China, therefore, dragons were regarded as friendly and helpful to mankind. Their powers were used to perform good deeds, which is a far different perception of dragons than most readers of fantasy fiction have come to know. Many

69

perceive dragons to be giant fire-breathing lizards based on what they have read in such books as the *Lord of the Rings* series by J.R.R. Tolkien, a British writer who was born in South Africa. Tolkien and other writers of fantasy have taken European myths and legends and embellished them to fit their stories. For example, in Tolkien's 1937 book, *The Hobbit*, he described the evil dragon Smaug:

> They had barely time to fly back to the tunnel, pulling and dragging in their bundles, when Smaug came hurtling from the North, licking the mountain-sides with flame, beating his great wings with a noise like a roaring wind. His hot breath shriveled the grass before the door, and drove in through the crack they had left and scorched them as they lay hid. Flickering fires leaped up and black rock-shadows danced. Then darkness fell as he passed again. The ponies screamed with terror, burst their ropes and galloped widely off. The dragon swooped and turned to pursue them, and was gone.[1]

Laurence Yep describes a much different type of dragon in his 1982 book, *Dragon of the Lost Sea,* as well as its three sequels, *Dragon Steel, Dragon Cauldron,* and *Dragon War*. In *Dragon of the Lost Sea*, the dragon, Shimmer, spends much of the book in the guise of an old beggar woman. Shimmer is more than just a dragon; she is a dragon princess. Her mission is to defeat an evil witch named Civet who has stolen the water of the Inland Sea, the home of the dragon clan. In Yep's books, the dragons are based on stories and images drawn from Chinese mythology rather than from familiar European legends.

Of course, Yep's readers know that he often makes references to dragons in his historical fiction, which includes *Dragonwings* and *Dragon's Gate*. In those books, there are no real dragons. Yep explains that he uses dragons in the titles for his historical fiction to provide a link between his books and traditional Chinese culture.

HOW A DRAGON FLIES

Yep may have made his mark as an author of historical fiction, but he began his career as an author of science fiction stories. He has continued to write in this genre, even as he churned out the books in the Golden Mountain Chronicles. Meanwhile, he has also written several books in the fantasy genre. Fantasy fiction typically features stories of dragons, as well as imps, unicorns, and other mythical creatures; it is regarded in literary circles as a close companion of science fiction. These two genres are closely related because they both ask readers to accept characters, images, and worlds that have very little or no basis in reality.

Despite this, the research Yep conducts for his fantasy and science fiction stories is often as thorough as the research he performs before he writes historical fiction. In fact, for *Dragon of the Lost Sea*, Yep did a lot more than just study about old Chinese myths in the library.

After he wrote a scene in the book describing the flight of a dragon, Yep concluded that the scene read too much like the flight scene in *Dragonwings*. Obviously, Yep knew that dragons do not resemble airplanes when they fly, so Yep decided to do some firsthand research in dragon flight: He hired a glider pilot.

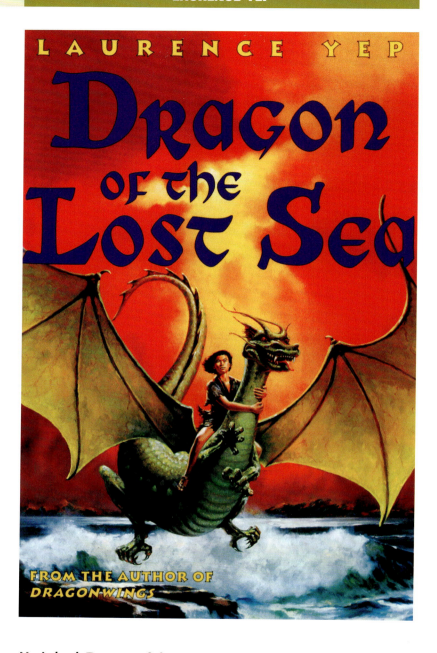

Yep's book Dragon of the Lost Sea *was published in 1982, after having been revised seven times. The story is based on a Chinese myth known as "Old Mother of the Waters."*

Yep decided that the flight of a dragon would probably be more like a glider than an airplane. The engineless gliders are towed aloft by an aircraft with an engine and then released. Once free of their towlines, the gliders float along on wind currents known as thermals, which rise and fall as the pilot catches each gust. Skilled glider pilots are able to ride thermals for hours and thereby keep their crafts aloft. As he recalled the flight, Yep said, "I would like to romanticize the experience for you, and tell you how inspiring and magnificent it was. However, it was really like a roller coaster ride without tracks."[2]

After making a variety of spins, loop-to-loops, and other maneuvers, Yep felt he had truly captured how it must feel for a dragon to soar through the sky. As he rode in the glider, however, he got very sick to his stomach, and he vowed to write about earth-bound characters in the future. Nevertheless, after he finished the glider flight, he was able to describe the flight of a dragon more precisely. He also felt that he had somehow made a connection with the mythological creatures. According to Yep, dragons "have also come to have a deeper meaning for me. They're symbols of my own creativity. Sometimes the dragon takes me where she wants to go rather than where I want to go. I think there's a dragon inside each of us."[3]

BUG-EYED MONSTERS

Whether he writes fantasy or science fiction stories, Yep believes he can make them more believable when the characters are more human. Yep said that he finds that much of the science fiction written today is dominated by "gadgetry,"[4] which means that a large portion of the book describes starships, laser cannons, super computers, and other devices the authors feel they must include in their plots. Very often, he believes, science fiction and fantasy authors neglect the human side of the story. As a result, Yep has given the aliens in his science fiction stories, as well as the dragons in his fantasy stories, very human qualities. He explains, "The thing about science fiction is being able to meet and confront aliens. They used to call them BEMs, or Bug Eyed Monsters—all the monster would do is try to devour you. But I wanted some friendly aliens, aliens that could help you, who'd not necessarily be completely superior in wisdom, but living their own kind of life."[5]

That is why Yep endows the character of Shimmer, the homeless dragon in *Dragon of the Lost Sea*, with human characteristics. In the book, Shimmer "adopts" an orphaned human named Thorn and says, "Well, we're family in a strange sort of way. I mean, heaven knows where my clan is because they're scattered all around the world, and you're an orphan. . . . And we already seem to have adopted one another."[6]

The dragon is not the only figure from Chinese myth that appears in Yep's fantasy stories. *Dragon of the Lost Sea* is based on a Chinese myth known as the "Old Mother of the Waters." When he researched the book, Yep learned about a Chinese folktale in which the Monkey King captures a spirit who has ordered a river to flood a village. In *Dragon of the Lost Sea*, Yep uses the character of the spirit in the book; he names her Civet and makes her the villain. The Monkey King plays a role, as well. The character of Thorn provides the human element to the story, and Shimmer becomes Thorn's protector.

Did you know...

The work of science-fiction writer Andre Norton helped inspire Laurence Yep to write his own stories and novels. Andre Norton's real name was Alice Mary Norton. Her first novel, *The Prince Commands*, was written in 1934. Shortly after that novel was published, she started to write under the name Andre because her publishers told her that young boys, who were her target audience, would be more willing to buy her books if they believed they were written by a man.

Norton was born in 1912 in Cleveland, Ohio. She attended college and planned to become a history teacher, but she was forced to drop out when she ran out of money. To help support her family, Norton took a job as a librarian, and she worked in libraries until 1958, when she became a full-time writer. By then, Norton had already written dozens of novels.

In 1963, she published *Witch World*, the first of more than 30 books in the series about the strange world where women wield magical powers. By the time she died in 2005, at the age of 93, Norton had written more than 130 novels and more than 100 short stories. She was also the editor of dozens of anthologies of science fiction and fantasy fiction.

Soon after Yep's *Sweetwater* was published, Norton paid her biggest fan a compliment when she praised the book. She wrote, "*Sweetwater* is outstanding. It is difficult to believe that this is a first novel. The extremely competent handling of alien background, plus excellent characterization, suggests rather a long apprenticeship in the craft."*

---

* Quoted in Joanne Ryder, "Laurence Yep," *Horn Book* 81, no. 4 (July–August 2005): p. 433.

Although Yep believes it is important to include the human element in fantasy and science fiction stories, he has not lost sight of the fact that the stories are, after all, about mythological beings, space aliens, and other creatures of his imagination. From the books of Andre Norton, Yep learned how important it is to not just tell a story and put words in the mouths of characters, but to actually create a world around them. As a result, he has always included details of the scenery and climate of the worlds in which his characters live. Said Yep, "It wasn't simply writing the story but creating the universe of the books that I've come to enjoy."[7]

Yep has also found that he does not have to stick solely to dragons and other characters of Chinese myth. He has taken the familiar myths, embellished them, and added his own characters to the stories. In *Dragon War*, the last book in the series, Yep introduces the character of the evil Boneless King, who is so vile that his flesh, lacking bones, creeps and slithers along the ground.

Dragon of the Lost Sea is an exciting adventure, as Shimmer and Thorn battle Civet to return the sea to the dragon clan. More important, it is also a story of friendship between the dragon and the boy that continues throughout the three sequels to *Dragon of the Lost Sea*. Each book sends Shimmer and Thorn on a new adventure; in fact, Yep hopes to write additional sequels to *Dragon of the Lost Sea*. He envisions a sequel in which Thorn has a romance, and he also plans to write a series of books in which the Monkey King will be the featured character.

TELLING HIS OWN STORY

Yep has never turned his back on science fiction, the first genre in which he found success. After the publication of

Sweetwater, Yep wrote *Seademons*, which also portrays a clash of cultures on a distant planet. This time, the planet Fancyfree is home to a people known as the Fair Folk and the Seademons, which are "large, squid-like animals that could communicate among themselves at what we thought was a primitive, animal level."[8] The Fair Folk and the Seademons are suspicious of one another until a catastrophe forces them to put aside their differences and work together.

For older readers, Yep has written *Shadow Lord*, a volume in the series of books based on the characters from the old *Star Trek* television show. In *Shadow Lord*, the two main characters are the Asian helmsman Sulu and the alien science officer Spock. Sulu and Spock are both outsiders who are particularly popular among *Star Trek* fans. Indeed, Yep believes the genre of science fiction appeals to its young fans because aliens are frequently outsiders, and many young people regard themselves as outsiders and outcasts. He said,

> By definition, adolescence is a period of feeling like an outsider. Teenagers are literally outsiders in their bodies because they are unable to stop or control the physical changes that are happening. They are also starting to develop their separate identities as individuals—which is a frightening, anxiety-generating enterprise. [When I once taught Mary Shelley's *Frankenstein* to a group of first-year university students, I was surprised when they identified not with . . . Dr. Frankenstein but with his monster.]
>
> I've continued to write about outsiders in my science fiction and fantasy as well. My *Star Trek* novel, *Shadow Lord*, is about Mr. Sulu and Mr. Spock, and I've centered my fantasy novels also on people and creatures who are on the margin of society.[9]

The use of Sulu as one of the main characters in *Shadow Lord* shows that Yep wants to use science fiction and fantasy novels to examine a familiar theme: the acceptance of Chinese people, and all Asians, into societies where they are regarded as outsiders. Sometimes, that experience can be related in humorous ways. In 1998, Yep published a fantasy novel titled *The Imp That Ate My Homework*. The book tells the story of a young Chinese-American boy named Jim who encounters a green, four-armed imp that causes him all manner of troubles, one of which, as the title suggests, is that he devoured Jim's homework. At wit's end, Jim approaches his mean and grumpy grandfather for advice on what to do about the imp. Jim has always been afraid of his grandfather and has never understood him or his ways. To his surprise, when Jim explains the situation to his grandfather, he tells Jim that he is actually a mythological being himself, a great hero who has chased the imp for centuries. His grandfather tells Jim the story of the imp and then enlists Jim's aid to trap the demon. In the book, the boy and his grandfather corner the demon in an old theater:

> I saw the imp standing in the middle of the stage. "After all these years, we can finally finish our feud," [Grandpop] sang. "Are you ready?" He seemed surprised to hear himself sing and felt his throat.
>
> Grandpop's cane changed to a sword. We he twirled it over his head, the blade shone in the theater lights. "You thought you were so clever to take the battle into the theater, but it's just what I planned," Grandpop sang back to the imp.[10]

Eventually, Jim and his grandfather defeat the imp. The whole experience awakens Jim's interest in Chinese culture and has given him new respect for his grandfather.

Although the story of a homework-eating imp may seem outlandish, it is not that much different than some of Yep's other novels. After all, in books as diverse as *Child of the Owl*, *Dragonwings*, and *The Imp That Ate My Homework*, Yep has told the story of young Americanized Chinese boys and girls who learn to accept and understand Chinese culture. Yep has told his own story in all of these books, even the one about the homework-munching imp.

The Mark Twain Murders *takes place in San Francisco in 1864. There, the main character of the novel, Duke Dougherty, meets up with Mark Twain, a down-on-his-luck reporter who has not yet made his mark as a famous novelist and essayist. The character is based on the real-life Mark Twain, shown above in 1907.*

San Francisco Mysteries

DUKE DOUGHERTY IS one of Laurence Yep's most unlikely heroes. Duke is not Chinese American but, rather, a homeless white boy who lives on the gritty San Francisco streets. Duke's father, Johnny, is murdered within the first few pages of Yep's book, *The Mark Twain Murders*, published in 1982. Duke does not have much affection for his father; in fact, he does not even believe that Johnny is his real father. Instead, Duke believes he is descended from European royalty and prefers to be known as "His Grace, the Duke of Baywater."

Duke soon meets up with Mark Twain, who has yet to make his mark as one of America's most renowned authors. Twain, whose real name was Samuel Clemens, is a down-on-his-luck newspaper reporter in San Francisco. It is 1864, toward the end of the Civil War. In Yep's story, Duke Dougherty and Mark Twain resolve to team up to find out the true story behind the murder of Johnny Dougherty.

Yep's first mystery, *The Mark Twain Murders* explores yet another literary genre. In the classic technique of most mystery writers, Yep presents the crime early in the book, then allows his two sleuths to learn the truth as they uncover a series of clues. Duke and Twain follow the trail of the killers to a stable, where Duke finds a piece of paper with a message scribbled on it:

> Mark came over excitedly. He took it between trembling fingers, trying not to crumble any more of the fragile paper. There, in plain script, it said: ". . . our raid on the M. . . ."
>
> He slipped the scrap protectively between two pages of his notebook and stowed it away inside a coat pocket. "What do you think the M stands for? M as in powder magazine—like the one at Black Point?"[1]

Soon, the two amateur detectives figure out that the M stands for the U.S. Mint in San Francisco, where the Union manufactures the gold and silver coins used for money in nineteenth-century America. More important, Duke and Twain uncover a Confederate plot to rob the mint.

In 1984, Yep followed *The Mark Twain Murders* with a sequel, *The Tom Sawyer Fires*. There is no question that the two books are mysteries, but they can also be included in the genre of historical fiction because Yep's research into the historical accuracy of the stories was rather extensive. For example, there truly was a plan by Confederate spies to rob the mint in San Francisco, but it was never carried out.

Mark Twain actually worked as a newspaper reporter in San Francisco in the 1860s. Yep also peppers the stories with other real-life characters. In *The Mark Twain Murders*, Twain and Duke encounter an eccentric street character who calls himself "Norton I, Emperor of the United States and Protector of Mexico." In fact, there was such a character: Joshua Abraham Norton, a wealthy Englishman who lost his money in a failed plot to buy up all the rice in San Francisco. Penniless, Norton moved into a cheap San Francisco hotel, where he declared himself emperor of the United States. A familiar figure on San Francisco streets, he became such a colorful character that the newspapers often published stories about his activities, and restaurant owners gladly gave him free meals. In the book, Duke, who also regards himself as a member of royalty, finds little humor in Norton's antics. He says,

> If you ask me, he gave a bad name to truly titled people who also were willing to earn their own living; but I wasn't in the mood for an argument. "Your Highness," I nodded to him.
>
> He lifted his head with imperial disdain and looked down at me. "Your Grace," he said, and strutted away.[2]

INSPIRED BY AN OLD PENNY

Another real-life character shows up in *The Tom Sawyer Fires*. The real Tom Sawyer was a San Francisco fireman, and that is how Yep portrays him in the book. In 1876, Twain published his novel, *The Adventures of Tom Sawyer*, about a young boy's antics in a small Missouri town. The novel became a landmark work of young people's fiction. Although there is no similarity between the young mischievous Tom Sawyer of fiction and the real-life Tom Sawyer,

Did you know...

Most people are familiar with Mark Twain's 1876 book, *The Adventures of Tom Sawyer*, which told the story of a mischievous boy from a small town in Missouri who fools his friends into whitewashing a fence, witnesses the evil Injun Joe commit a murder, and finds treasure buried in a cave.

There was a real Tom Sawyer, though, who emerges as a character in Laurence Yep's book, *The Tom Sawyer Fires*. The real Tom Sawyer may have known Mark Twain when the author lived in San Francisco and worked for a newspaper. In fact, Sawyer's deeds may have inspired Twain to envision him as the plucky boy hero he depicted in his book.

Born in New York City in 1832, Sawyer held a number of odd jobs until he signed on as a sailor. Sawyer worked as a fireman aboard ships, which means that he shoveled coal into the steam engines that powered the vessels. On one voyage, his steamship, the *Independence*, struck a reef and sunk. Sawyer escaped and is given credit for saving the lives of 90 of the passengers.

In 1859, Sawyer gave up the sailor's life to settle in San Francisco, where he worked as a policeman and saloon keeper. He also became a volunteer fireman, which is probably how he met Mark Twain. As a reporter, Twain was obviously dispatched many times to cover fires.

many historians are convinced that Twain knew Sawyer in San Francisco and borrowed his name for the book.

Yep also includes a true incident in *The Tom Sawyer Fires*. When he lived in San Francisco, Twain had a lot of respect for the Chinese and was appalled by the way whites treated them. Later, in his 1872 book, *Roughing It,* which told the story of his life in the West, Twain wrote that the Chinese "are a great convenience to everybody—even to the worst class of white men, for he bears the most of their sins, suffering fines for their petty thefts, imprisonment for their robberies, and death for their murders."[3] In *Roughing It*, Twain reports the case of an elderly Chinese man who was stoned to death by San Francisco boys, "and that although a large crowd witnessed the shameful deed, no one interfered."[4]

In fact, Twain witnessed the death of a Chinese man killed by whites, and he wrote a story about the murder. When his newspaper refused to publish the piece, Twain quit in protest. In *The Tom Sawyer Fires*, Duke asks Twain about the incident, and the author responds, "I quit on a matter of principle. They wouldn't publish a story I'd done about a Chinese man getting beaten up while a policeman watched. . . . And that's the pure unadulterated truth."[5]

In the two mysteries, Yep draws a gritty portrait of San Francisco, which he presents as dirty and corrupt. This is a pivotal time for San Francisco as it tries to rid itself of its wide-open reputation for gambling and wild behavior and become a respectable modern city of the American West. Yep portrays the city in the midst of change while he also weaves stories of suspense into the two books.

According to Yep, these books were inspired by his love for mystery stories, as well as his desire to write about San Francisco during the Civil War era. Yep said he conceived the idea for writing about that era of life in San Francisco from an old penny he carries around. As a boy, while he worked in the family store, Yep sold groceries to a customer who paid his bill with some loose change. As he examined the coins before he put them in the cash register, Yep discovered that he had been given an old penny minted in San Francisco in 1864. The penny was made of bronze rather than copper because copper was in a short supply during the war. Of course, the penny did not include an image of President Lincoln, who was still alive when it was made. (Lincoln's image was not added to the penny until 1909). Instead, the image on the face of the coin was that of an Indian head.

Over the years, Yep kept the old penny. As he wrote *The Mark Twain Murders*, Yep came across the failed plot to rob the U.S. Mint in San Francisco. He took the old penny out of his pocket and put it on his desk, where it could serve as a daily reminder of life in 1864 San Francisco.

SUPPORTING ROLES

In 1997, Yep introduced a new mystery series. Once again, the mysteries were centered in San Francisco, but this time Yep featured Chinese Americans as his main characters. He also set the books in a contemporary period of time, which means that the stories did not rely on historical events.

Still, *The Case of the Goblin Pearls* and its two sequels, *The Case of the Lion Dance* and *The Case of the Fire-crackers*, do call attention to a few pages from Chinese-American history. For example, Yep examines the obstacles that Chinese Americans had to overcome to gain recognition as entertainers on stage and in the movies. In these

In The Case of the Goblin Pearls, *Yep pays tribute to Anna May Wong, the first major Chinese-American actress. Wong, shown above in 1932, appeared in many movies, in which she often played a house-keeper, cook, or other supporting role.*

three books, one of the main characters is an aging actress, Tiger Lil, who helps her young niece, Lily Lew, solve a series of crimes in their Chinatown neighborhood.

Yep based the character of Tiger Lil on a number of his mother's friends, but at the end of *The Case of the Goblin Pearls* he pays tribute to the actress Anna May Wong, Hollywood's first major Chinese-American actress. He indicates that the character of Tiger Lil was, at least in part, based on Wong. Although Wong was a very successful actress who appeared in many movies, she never achieved the same level of stardom that white actresses enjoyed in Hollywood during the 1930s and 1940s. Even worse, she was often forced to play supporting roles, and she was frequently cast as a housekeeper or cook.

Other Asian actors and actresses shared Wong's plight. In fact, during the 1930s and 1940s, Hollywood studios produced a very popular series of films that featured the fictional Honolulu detective Charlie Chan. The films were based on a series of Charlie Chan mysteries written by American author Earl Derr Biggers, who described his detective as a Chinese American. Yet, the Hollywood studios chose to cast white actors made up to look Chinese to portray the detective, although Chinese-American actors were always cast for the films' supporting roles.

In *The Case of the Goblin Pearls*, the Lew family learns that Chinese-American actors were often frozen out of substantial film roles. Yep emphasizes this in the beginning of the story, when Lily and her family watch videotapes of their aunt's movies. Lily soon realizes that Tiger Lil appears in few scenes in the films. Lily says, "The trouble was that Auntie usually had only one scene. . . . She was funny, but she didn't have much time on camera, and she almost always seemed to be a maid."[6]

Sweatshops are businesses that often employ new immigrants desperate for work. The word sweatshop describes the poor working conditions usually present in such businesses, such as the one shown above in New York city in 1908.

Lily and her aunt soon team up and become amateur sleuths. In *The Case of the Goblin Pearls*, Lily and Tiger Lil track down pearls stolen from a Chinatown sweatshop by a masked robber. Sweatshops are businesses that usually employ new immigrants desperate for work. In most cases, the sweatshops manufacture garments and mostly employ women to sew. The women are typically crammed tightly into basements or back rooms and forced to work long hours for little money.

Today, sweatshops are illegal because state and federal laws require employees to earn the minimum wage, which is more than five dollars an hour. Most cities and states, as well as the federal government, dictate how many workers can occupy a building, which guarantees workers' safety. Still, there is little doubt that illegal sweatshops exist. New immigrants are often desperate for money and are willing to work for sweatshop wages, which may be just a few dollars a day. In *The Case of the Goblin Pearls*, Lily finds her way to the Happy Fortune sweatshop:

> I had passed by sweatshops all my life, but it was the first time I'd ever been in one. Light bulbs hung down from the ceiling, but there weren't enough, so it was dim inside there, and stuffy, too. I couldn't have read there, let alone sewed. Ringing the room were wheeled iron clothing racks bulging with clothes. There was a space between two racks, and through it I saw a door labeled "Office." In a space between two other racks, I saw an open door leading to the solitary toilet.[7]

Lily goes on to describe the conditions in the sweatshop. She finds 20 sewing machines in the room and sees that the women who work at the machines are forced to sit jammed together, with narrow aisles that separate the machines. She learns that the women can earn 50 cents for a blouse that sells for $80 in a downtown store, and that some of the women work 10 or 12 hours a day, 7 days a week.

In the story, Lily helps expose the illegal conditions she found in the Happy Fortune sweatshop. According to Yep, the Happy Fortune itself is fictional, but "unfortunately the working conditions are not. It is a shameful, ongoing abuse."[8]

Above, Mao Zedong, leader of China from 1954 until his death in 1976, reviews the Red Guards in Beijing in 1966. The Red Guard plays a role in Laurence Yep's novel Angelfish, *in which an influential character reveals that he had been a famous ballet dancer in China before he ran afoul of the Red Guards.*

8

Stories About Families

FROM 1966 UNTIL 1976, a group of thugs known as the Red Guards virtually ruled China. Chinese Communist leader Mao Zedong gave them free rein to uncover his enemies and drive them out of power. By no means did the Red Guards limit themselves to Mao's immediate rivals; they regarded those with contrary ideas to be enemies of the state. Anyone in a position of influence was rounded up, fired, thrown into prison, tortured, or driven out of the country; this included college professors, scientists, artists, and entertainers. In Chinese history, this period is known as the Cultural Revolution. In the 10 years of the Cultural Revolution, it is believed that millions of Chinese citizens fell victim to the strong-arm tactics of the Red Guards.

In *Angelfish*, published in 2001, a young ballet student named Robin Lee finds a job in a tropical fish store in her Chinatown neighborhood. Mr. Cao, who is quite grumpy, owns the store. Although Mr. Cao seems to know a lot about ballet and gives Robin an ointment to help a leg injury heal, for the most part he is impatient with her and constantly complains about the quality of her work.

Eventually, Robin learns the truth: Mr. Cao had been a famous ballet star in China, but he ran afoul of the Red Guards. He was captured, paraded through the streets as a traitor to the communist regime, tortured, and fired from the ballet. In the story, Robin asks her Auntie Ruby,

> "But what did the dancers do wrong? We just try to give people pleasure."
>
> "Dancers were also part of the elite." Auntie Ruby shrugged. "They were parasites living off the workers."
>
> It was like hearing about a horror movie. In this case, though, it wasn't just a few people who were destroyed, but a whole nation.[1]

CONTEMPORARY DRAMAS

The communist government has been in power in China since 1949, when the communists under Mao defeated Chiang Kai-shek's nationalist forces and drove them to the nearby island of Taiwan. For nearly the next three decades, Mao presided over a ruthless regime. Under Mao, the state took complete control of the lives of all mainland Chinese, a situation that intensified during the years of the Cultural Revolution.

Mao died in 1976, but the communist regime has continued to rule China with an iron fist. In 1989, the government violently suppressed an uprising in Beijing's Tiananmen Square, where students demonstrated for rights and freedoms denied them under the communists. It is believed that government forces killed as many as 2,600 Chinese people, mostly students, who refused to disperse. Today, the government continues to monitor the activities of the people very closely. In China, dissent is not tolerated.

Many Chinese Americans therefore believe little has changed in China since the days of the Cultural Revolution. Said Yep, "Mr. Cao is fictional, but the excesses of the Cultural Revolution have been widely documented."[2]

What sets *Angelfish* apart from most of Yep's other books is not what the book is about, but what it is not about. It is not a science fiction story that features alien civilizations or a fantasy story with a dragon in disguise as an old beggar woman. It is not a story drawn from an event of historical significance, although Mr. Cao's experiences in the Cultural Revolution are certainly an important part of the story. Finally, Yep does not include a mystery for his amateur sleuths to solve. Instead, *Angelfish* is set in contemporary times and examines the lives of a modern Chinese-American family. It is simply a story about a young ballet student's struggles to understand her culture and her family.

Yep has, in fact, written several similar contemporary dramas. His other works in the genre include *Ribbons* and its sequel, *The Cook's Family*; *The Amah*; and *Kind Hearts and Gentle Monsters*. These books include some familiar Yep themes: Chinese-American protagonists have been assimilated into American society, and then they learn about their heritage and culture from older characters.

One contemporary drama that does include an element of mystery is Yep's *Liar, Liar*, which was published in

1983. In the book, the protagonist is not a Chinese American, but a white teenager named Sean, who is out to prove that the death of his friend Marsh was not an accident. He believes that it was engineered by an adult, Russ Towers, in

Did you know...

Laurence Yep has written books for adult and teen readers, as well as for preteens. He has also written books for readers as young as four years old.

Among his books for beginning readers are *The Boy Who Swallowed Snakes*, a storybook about a boy named Little Chou who figures out that the best way to defeat poisonous snakes is to eat them. Since Little Chou has a pure heart, the poison does not harm him.

According to Yep, he came across the myth that inspired the story as he researched another book. He said there are "treasures to be discovered in folklore—sometimes hidden in the tiniest type in the dullest scholarly footnotes—such as the story of the boy who escaped deadly, magical snakes not by fighting them or fleeing them but by the uniquely Chinese strategy of eating them for dinner."*

The Shell Woman and the King, another book for beginning readers, tells the story of a fisherman named Uncle Wu. He marries a beautiful girl who can change herself from a shell into a human, and she uses her power to defeat an evil tyrant. Yep explores a similar theme in *The Man Who Tricked a Ghost*, in which a young boy named Sung outwits a ghost when he spits on it.

* Laurence Yep, "Wilder Medal Acceptance," *Horn Book* 81, no. 4 (July–August 2005): p. 429.

retribution for a prank that Marsh played on him. As it turns out, Towers hates all teenagers because a teenage driver killed his wife and child. Sean proves that Towers not only caused Marsh's death but also is responsible for many other "accidents." Still, in *Liar, Liar*, Sean's strained relationships with his family and friends are clearly the engine that drives the story.

FOOT BINDING

Angelfish is actually the third of Yep's books to feature the ballet student Robin Lee. She made her first appearance in *Ribbons*, Yep's 1992 book. Robin is forced to give up dancing to care for her grandmother, who has emigrated from Hong Kong. At first, Robin is bitter, but she soon forms a bond with her grandmother. Robin's feet have grown into unnatural shapes due to the stress of ballet training. One day, she notices her grandmother's feet are also misshapen:

> I got a nasty jolt when I opened the door. Grandmother was sitting fully clothed on the edge of the bathtub. Her pants were rolled up to her knees, and she had her feet soaking in a pan of water.
>
> "Don't you know how to knock?" she snapped, and reached for a towel.
>
> "You usually lock the door," I said indignantly.
>
> She tried to drop the towel over her feet, but she wasn't quick enough because I saw her bare feet for the first time. It was as if her feet were like taffy that someone had stretched out and twisted. They bent downward in a way that feet were not meant to, and her toes stuck up at odd angles, more like lumps than toes. I didn't think she had all ten either. [3]

Robin's grandmother had been a victim of "foot binding," a custom practiced in China since the fourteenth century.

Girls were subjected to this as young as three years old. First, all the toes except the girl's two big toes were broken. Then, her feet were bound tightly with ribbons to keep them from growing larger than about four inches. It was believed that girls with smaller feet were better dancers.

Sadly, foot binding forced girls' feet to grow into unnatural shapes. As they grew older, the girls experienced more and more pain from having had their feet bound tightly with ribbons. Most of them became crippled as older women. Although foot binding was officially outlawed in China in 1911, the practice continued in some areas. There are many women like Robin's grandmother whose feet are misshapen; in fact, Chinese shoe factories continue to manufacture special shoes for elderly women who suffer from the effects of foot binding.

Robin's story continues in *The Cook's Family*. Robin and her grandmother grow closer amid the turmoil of Robin's home life, which has deteriorated as her parents argue and drift further apart. To escape the constant bickering at home, Robin and her grandmother find jobs at a Chinese restaurant, where they encounter a lonely old cook named Wolf with no family of his own. They pretend to be related to Wolf, and he accepts them warmly:

> Wolf and Grandmother chatted on. All he'd really wanted was an excuse to talk about his family.
>
> And I felt as if Grandmother had opened a window just a crack so I could see into her world. I suppose if I was seven thousand miles away from China, I might like to talk with someone who shared the same kind of past.
>
> It's a funny thing about fantasy. When three people share it, it doesn't seem as crazy. And it doesn't seem nearly as fragile.[4]

In *The Cook's Family*, Yep returned to a theme he examined in *Dragonwings*: the plight of men from China who were forced to leave their families behind when they immigrated to the United States. Wolf was one such émigré. Yep conceived the idea of a substitute family after he read about a practice in Japan in which sons and daughters who are too busy to visit their elderly parents hire actors to make the visits. The elderly parents are quite aware that they are actors, and not their children, who visit them. They are so lonely, however, that they accept the actors as their own flesh and blood. After he read about the make-believe sons and daughters in Japan, Yep said he could understand how a lonely old cook like Wolf would also be willing to accept a substitute family. Of course, the relationship also holds a lot of significance for Robin, who is at a point in her life when she needs a strong family but is unable to find one at home.

GODZILLA AND THE UGLY STEPSISTER

Another young ballet dancer, Amy Chin, is at the center of *The Amah*. Amy faces some changes in her life when her father dies and her mother is forced to work as an *amah*, which is a nanny. Amy must care for her own brothers and sisters, which gives her less time for ballet lessons. She also finds that she has grown apart from her family, and she thinks that they have more love for Stephanie, the young rich girl for whom their mother cares, than they do for Amy. In the story, Amy says,

> Up until now when I read the Cinderella story, I had always sympathized with her and hated her stepsisters. Now I knew how Cinderella's stepsisters felt. Cinderella could do no wrong. They could do no right. She was beautiful. They were ugly. Everyone loved Cinderella and no one loved them.

Suddenly, it hit me. In my own life story, I wasn't Cinderella. I was a stepsister.[5]

Yep often writes about outsiders who try to fit in. In *Kind Hearts and Gentle Monsters*, he gives that familiar theme an unusual twist. The book tells the story of a blossoming romance between Charlie and Chris, who are two vastly different personalities. Charlie is an athlete and a good student and he is active in school activities. Chris is a rebellious girl who has discipline problems. In this case, Chris is clearly the outsider, but unlike other Yep characters, she makes no effort to fit in. Instead, she criticizes Charlie; she thinks he is too rigid and does not leave room for other ideas. She says, "Why is it that everything that doesn't fit into your nice, white, Catholic, middle-class mold is *always* sick or weird?"[6]

Yep received some of his inspiration for *Kind Hearts and Gentle Monsters* after he talked to school students in Seattle, Washington. During the visit, Yep told the students how much he loved to watch the old Japanese-produced movies about the mythological monster Godzilla. Yep wondered whether there would be any more movies because he had recently learned that the actor who played Godzilla had retired. He recalled,

A little boy piped up from the back of the room, "You mean there's an actor who plays Godzilla?"

I felt as if I had killed Santa Claus and the Easter Bunny all in one blow.[7]

That exchange prompted Yep to include a young character in the book named Duane, who is a big fan of Godzilla movies. In the book, Duane confides that he loves Godzilla "because you can put him anywhere and he'll always survive—even win and make new friends."[8] It is a lesson that

Laurence Yep is a fan of the old Japanese movies that featured the myth-ical monster Godzilla, who is shown above in the 1954 film Godzilla, King of the Monsters! *In Yep's novel* Kind Hearts and Gentle Mon-sters, *a main character also professes to be a great fan of Godzilla.*

Charlie and Chris eventually learn to apply to themselves and to each other. The original title for the book was *Yes Virginia, There Is a Godzilla*, but Yep and his publisher could not con-vince the Japanese movie company that owns the rights to the monster's name to let them borrow it for Yep's book.

Kind Hearts and Gentle Monsters, *The Amah*, *The Cook's Family*, and many other books prove that Laurence Yep does not need a space alien, a dragon, a mystery, or a famous event in the history of China to tell a good story. He only needs strong characters like Charlie, Chris, Robin Lee, and Amy Chin.

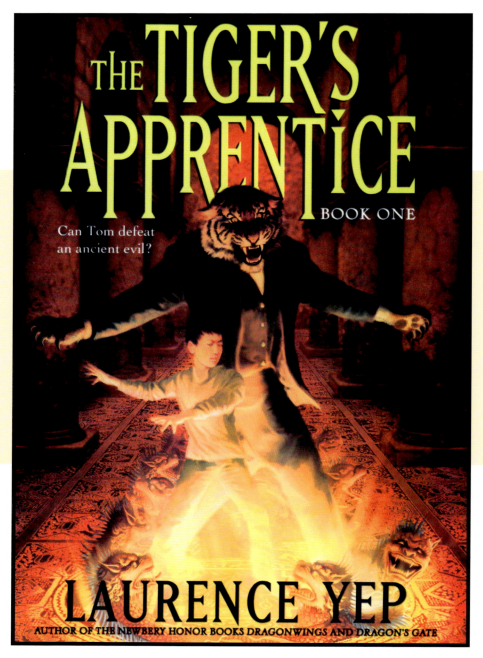

THE TIGER'S APPRENTICE

Can Tom defeat
an ancient evil?

BOOK ONE

LAURENCE YEP

AUTHOR OF THE NEWBERY HONOR BOOKS DRAGONWINGS AND DRAGON'S GATE

In ancient Chinese tradition, the tiger is regarded as a rival of the dragon and is admired for its strength and ferociousness. With 2003's The Tiger's Apprentice, *Yep began a new trilogy that focuses on the mythological power of the tiger.*

9

New Stories to Tell

IT IS TRUE that the dragon is an important symbol of Chinese mythology and culture, but there are other symbols, as well. The tiger is one such symbol. Regarded as a rival to the dragon, the ancient Chinese admired the tiger for its strength and ferociousness. "Tigers may not be as powerful as dragons but they can be far friendlier," said Yep. "Tigers will disguise themselves and live among humans and even join their families in various ways."[1]

In 2003, Yep wrote his first book in a new three-book series that examines the mythological powers of the tiger. In a return to the fantasy genre, Yep published *The Tiger's Apprentice*, in which Tom, a young Chinese-American boy, teams up with a magical tiger named Mr. Hu. Together, they protect a phoenix egg that could cause worldwide havoc if it falls into the wrong hands.

In the story, Mr. Hu is a "Guardian," a member of an ancient order of tigers who must guard the eggs of the phoenix. Tom, a magic student who has grown up in San Francisco's Chinatown, is his reluctant apprentice. Early in the story, Tom meets the shape-shifting Mr. Hu:

> The stranger looked like an elderly man with a trim, gray mustache and goatee—except for his furry ears. The stranger brushed his goatee. "Do I have something on my face? Is that why you're staring?"
>
> Tom's grandmother had taught him some basic spells, and one of them was for showing the true shape of things—which she said was essential for anyone working in magic. Curious about his grandmother's visitor, Tom chanted the words under his breath. He jumped when the next instant he saw a tiger standing there on his hind legs.[2]

The phoenix, otherwise known as the firebird, is a mythological bird that is said to possess great powers. The most widely known story about the phoenix is its ability to rise from the dead. Once it dies and is consumed by fire, a new phoenix will emerge from the ashes. This myth has evolved over time in folktales told in Western cultures. As with many myths, the Chinese have their own version. Said Yep, "I was struck by the fact that the Chinese phoenix had the power to change bad creatures. I wondered if the reverse were true: if a phoenix could also have the power to change good creatures. That was the seed from which this book grew."[3]

Yep has written two sequels: *Tiger's Blood*, which was published in 2005, and *Tiger Magic*, which was published in 2006. In each book, Tom and Mr. Hu must continue a centuries-old battle against the forces of evil to protect the egg and the young magical bird that is eventually hatched. Their struggle takes place in many far-off and mystical places, such as the kingdom of the dragons, which is miles below the surface of the earth. Tom and Mr. Hu, however, never leave Chinatown. The world of the Guardians exists on the streets and in the alleys of Chinatown, albeit in a parallel world that Yep has created. To an ordinary person, life goes on as usual, but to Tom and Mr. Hu, the streets are filled with such creatures as Kung Kung, a snake with a human face; Mistral, a dragon; and Monkey, a golden ape. Said Yep, "Though San Francisco appears normal to the average person, the battle for the phoenix begins again in the alleys and foggy streets and the boy finds himself in the middle of a new shadow war."[4]

The trilogy has proven to be popular among Yep's fans, and it may serve to provide Yep with his widest audience ever. Yep has sold the rights to produce the series in a film version to the movie company Miramax. Producer Jane Startz, who turned such classic children's stories as *The Indian in the Cupboard* and *The Baby-Sitter's Club* into film versions, will head the project for Miramax. She said, "I have been a fan of the author Laurence Yep for a very long time and I think this is one of those really special children's fantasies that's got heart and scope and is very cinematic."[5] No release date for the film version of *The Tiger's Apprentice* has been set.

DILEMMA OF THE OUTSIDER

Like most of Yep's books, there is a familiar theme in *The Tiger's Apprentice*: Tom is an outsider drawn into a world of shape-shifting tigers, phoenixes, and other magical creatures. Indeed, it is a theme that Yep has woven through most of his more than 60 novels and other books. In 2005, the Association for Library Services to Children, which is a division of the American Library Association, recognized his lifelong efforts to chronicle the obstacles faced by outsiders. The group presented him with the Laura Ingalls Wilder Medal for his lifetime of work in which he chronicled "the dilemma of the cultural outsider,"[6] according to Janice M. Del Negro, chairwoman of the committee that confers the award.

Laura Ingalls Wilder is one of the most revered names in children's literature. She was the author of many works of historical fiction about pioneer life on the plains; her most famous work is *Little House on the Prairie*. Indeed, the medal awarded in her name is one of the highest honors that can be bestowed on an author of young people's literature. Other winners of the award have included E.B. White, author of the classic children's story *Charlotte's Web*; Maurice Sendak, author of the well-known *Where the Wild Things Are*; and Theodor S. Geisel, who is more widely known by his pen name, Dr. Seuss. "I never expected to be in such company as the previous winners of the Laura Ingalls Wilder Medal," said Yep.[7]

DEVASTATION OF AN EARTHQUAKE

The Tiger's Apprentice books marked Yep's return as a fantasy fiction writer. He has also continued to write historical fiction with the publication of *The Earth Dragon Awakes: The San Francisco Earthquake of 1906*. Published in 2006 on the one hundredth anniversary of the earthquake, the book tells the story of two young San Francisco boys, Henry Travis and Chinese immigrant Chin, the son of the

Did you know...

For younger readers, Laurence Yep has written a series that illustrates his sense of humor. *Later Gator*; *Cockroach Cooties*; and *Skunk Scout* tell of the adventures of Teddy, a 10-year-old Chinese-American boy who continually looks for ways to annoy his little brother, Bobby.

According to Yep, the stories are based very much on his own experiences growing up in San Francisco. For example, in *Later Gator*, Teddy's mother sends him to the pet store to buy a pet turtle for his little brother's birthday. Instead, Teddy buys a baby alligator that he hopes will horrify his little brother. The alligator fails to scare Bobby, who becomes attached to the critter, and Teddy learns to love the alligator, too. The only problem is that baby alligators soon grow into huge beasts, so Teddy and Bobby have to figure out a way to keep the alligator at home. Yep said the incident actually happened in his house, except he is the one who brought home the pet alligator in an attempt to scare his older brother, Tom.

The other stories include *Cockroach Cooties*, in which Teddy and Bobby adopt a pet cockroach they use to scare the school bully, and *Skunk Scout*, in which Teddy and Bobby are forced to endure a weekend camping trip with their Uncle Curtis, who is not much of an outdoorsman.

Published in 2006 on the one hundredth anniversary of the earthquake,
The Earth Dragon Awakes: The San Francisco Earthquake of
1906, *tells the story of two young San Francisco boys, Henry Travis*
and Chinese immigrant Chin, as they endure the devastation of the
earthquake, some of which is shown above in this 1906 photograph.

houseboy in the Travis home, as they endure the devastation of the earthquake.

San Francisco is located near the San Andreas Fault, a geological formation that is prone to shifts in the surface of the earth. When the surface near the fault shifts, an earthquake occurs. As a result, San Francisco and other California communities face constant danger from earthquakes.

Indeed, many residents of the city have lived through the scary and destructive quakes. In 1957, Yep was attending school in San Francisco when a large quake hit the city and shook the building. In 1989, a massive quake caused millions of dollars in damage. Yep and his wife Joanne were trapped in the city that day; there was no electricity, so they had to follow the news of the disaster on a battery-powered radio.

The worst earthquake in the city's history, though, occurred on April 18, 1906. The earthquake caused great devastation, but the worst was yet to come. At the time, most of the homes and other buildings were constructed of wood. People often cooked over open fires, and homes were heated by fire, or by gas, which is highly flammable. Outside, the streetlamps were also lit by gas. The earthquake caused a huge fire to break out; within a day, the fire destroyed whatever the earthquake had not leveled. In all, some 28,000 homes, businesses, and other buildings were destroyed. More important, as many as 3,600 people are believed to have perished in the quake and the subsequent fire.

On April 19, 1906, Yep's grandfather returned to the city after a visit home. He arrived to find San Francisco engulfed in flames. Instead of leaving the ship, the Chinese Americans on board were detained for a week on Angel Island in San Francisco Bay. Angel Island served as an immigration station for Chinese immigrants and other Asian people who wished to enter the United States. It fulfilled the same purpose on the West Coast as Ellis Island served on the East Coast.

Indeed, the Chinese people of San Francisco suffered greatly from the aftershocks of the earthquake, as well as from the fire. Already abused and the victims of prejudice, many Chinese people were barred from the little available housing by white landlords, who wanted to make sure the housing went to white people first. Instead, Chinese-Americans were forced to live in camps, where the only available shelter was a tent or a shack. Chinatown was rebuilt in the same neighborhood where it had been located before the disaster. In *The Earth Dragon Awakes*, Yep describes the devastation that hit the city:

> More books spill out of the bookcase. The chest of drawers dances a jig. The walls groan. The wooden floor ripples like waves of an ocean. Windows rattle. Doors thump in their frames. . . .
>
> Plates crash in the kitchen below. Pictures and then plaster drop from the wall. Old boards show through the gaps. Henry coughs in the growing cloud of dust.
>
> And still the shaking goes on. His bed and all his furniture circle in a slow waltz around the room.
>
> Then the window shatters. The shade flies up with a flap. The other houses in the neighborhood jerk about. Immediately across the street, the Smiths' house falls apart. Bricks rain on the ground. Dust rises and hides the street. From within the cloud, Henry hears screams.[8]

RETURN TO ANGEL ISLAND

As with all of his historical fiction, Yep has taken great pains to ensure that the details of the earthquake are accurate. He researched the earthquake for months and consulted numerous sources. In fact, at the end of the book, he even includes photographs of the city shot during the earthquake and the fire.

In 2007, Yep published *Dragon Road*, a work of historical fiction based on the real-life exploits of a Chinese-American basketball team that barnstormed across the United States in 1939 and 1940. The team once played the Harlem Globetrotters, the famous team of African-American basketball stars known for their humorous antics on the court. Yep has begun work on a nonfiction book titled *Angel Island: Conversations with My Father*. As he dramatized in *Dragonwings*, Yep's father, Thomas, arrived at Angel Island in 1924. He was one of the 175,000 Chinese immigrants who were detained at Angel Island from the time the facility opened in 1910 until it closed some 30 years later. About his research for the project, Yep said, "The National Archives has over 400 pages of interviews and photos of my father's family. It includes an interview with my father when he was only 10 years old. It's like having a time machine that lets me listen to my father when he was a child."[9]

At this point in his career, Laurence Yep has many projects in the works, which means that children will have an opportunity to read his novels and other books for many years to come. Whether he chooses to write science fiction, fantasy, historical fiction, mystery, or stories of contemporary life, Yep's readers have learned to expect strong stories that feature courageous people. Nevertheless, the characters in Yep's books are willing to learn lessons about themselves, as well as the cultures of their ancestors. As he looked back on his 30-year career as an author of books for young readers, Yep said,

> Whether it's science fiction, fantasy, historical fiction, mysteries or contemporary realism, I have one main theme in my writing, and I learned that lesson both in my African American neighborhood and in Chinatown: A person's true value can be measured neither by a bank account nor by titles but by that person's heart; and I have been privileged to meet people, both in person and in books, who have led lives of quiet heroism and who rose to the occasion when challenged.[10]

CHRONOLOGY

1909   Fung Joe Guey flies a homemade biplane near Oakland, California; the flight will inspire Yep to write *Dragonwings*.

1915   The family of Yep's mother, Franche Lee, arrives in the United States.

1924   Yep's father, Thomas, arrives at the Angel Island immigration station in San Francisco Bay.

1948   Laurence Yep is born in San Francisco on June 14.

1950s   Yep grows up in San Francisco, where he reads the Oz series of books, as well as books written by science fiction writer Andre Norton.

1966   Yep graduates from high school and enrolls as a journalism student at Marquette University in Milwaukee, Wisconsin.

1968   Yep's first short story, "The Selchey Kids," is published in a national science-fiction magazine; he changes his major to English and transfers to the University of California–Santa Cruz.

1970   Yep is graduated from college and begins to teach English at the State University of New York at Buffalo.

1973   Yep's first novel, *Sweetwater*, is published.

1975   *Dragonwings* is published.

1976   *Dragonwings* is selected as a Newbery Honor Book.

1977   *Child of the Owl* and *Seademons* are published.

1979   *Sea Glass* is published.

1982   *Dragon of the Lost Sea* and *The Mark Twain Murders* are published.

1984   *The Serpent's Children* and *The Tom Sawyer Fires* are published.

1991   *The Star Fisher* is published.

1992   *Ribbons* is published.

1993 *Dragon's Gate* is published; the book is selected as a Newbery Honor Book.

1997 *The Case of the Goblin Pearls* is published.

1998 *The Imp That Ate My Homework* is published.

2001 *Angelfish* is published.

2003 *The Tiger's Apprentice* is published.

2005 *Tiger's Blood* is published; Yep is awarded the Laura Ingalls Wilder Medal.

2006 *Tiger Magic* and *The Earth Dragon Awakes: The San Francisco Earthquake of 1906* are published.

2007 *Dragon Road* is published.

NOTES

Chapter 1

1 Quoted in Pamela S. Dear, ed., *Contemporary Authors: New Revision Series*, vol. 46. Detroit, Mich.: Gale Research, 1995, p. 480.

2 Laurence Yep, *Dragonwings*. New York: Scholastic, 1975, pp. 11–12.

3 Laurence Yep, "Writing Dragonwings," *Reading Teacher* 30, no. 4 (January 1977): pp. 359–363; reprinted in Diane Johnson-Feelings, *Presenting Laurence Yep*. New York: Twayne, 1995, pp. 101–102.

4 Yep, *Dragonwings*, pp. 31–32.

5 Laurence Yep, *The Lost Garden*. New York: Julian Messner, 1991, p. 5.

6 Yep, *Dragonwings*, p. 237.

7 Quoted in Scot Peacock, ed., *Something About the Author*, vol. 123. Farmington Hills, Mich.: Gale Group, 2001, p. 194.

8 HarperCollins interview with Laurence Yep about *The Traitor*. www.harpercollins .com/authorintro/index .asp?authorid=12929.

9 Quoted in Donna Olendorg, ed., *Something About the Author*, vol. 69. Detroit, Mich.: Gale Research, 1992, p. 232.

Chapter 2

1 Yep, *The Lost Garden*, p. 13.

2 Ibid., p. 16.

3 Laurence Yep, "I Have a Watch," speech given at the University of California–Davis School of Education, Jan. 19, 2005, p. 2.

4 Quoted in Peacock, ed., *Something About the Author*, vol. 123, p. 193.

5 Quoted in Leonard S. Marcus, "Talking With Authors," *Publishers Weekly* 247, no. 7 (February 14, 2000): p. 98.

6 Yep, *The Lost Garden*, p. 78.

7 Ibid., p. 99.

8 Ibid., p. 101.

9 Quoted in Joanne Ryder, "Laurence Yep," *Horn Book* 81, no. 4 (July–August 2005): p. 433.

Chapter 3

1 Quoted in Scot Peacock, ed., *Contemporary Authors: New Revision Series*. vol. 92. Farmington Hills, Mich.: Thomson Gale, 2001, p. 461.

2 Quoted in Diane Johnson-Feelings, *Presenting Laurence Yep*. New York: Twayne, 1995, p. 22.

3 Quoted in Marcus, "Talking with Authors."

4 Ibid.

5 Laurence Yep, *Dragonwings*. New York: Scholastic, 1977, pp. 247–248.

6 Passage from *Child of the Owl*, reprinted in Donna E. Norton, *Through the Eyes of a Child: An Introduction to Children's Literature*. Columbus, Ohio: Charles E. Merrill, 1983, p. 518.

7 Passage from *Sea Glass*, reprinted in Johnson-Feelings, *Presenting Laurence Yep*, p. 75.

8 Laurence Yep, *The Star Fisher*. New York: Morrow Junior, 1991, p. viii.

Chapter 4

1 Laurence Yep, "True Heroes," *Horn Book Magazine* 78, no. 6 (November–December 2002): p. 792.

2 Quoted in Cecelia Goodnow, "For Inspiration, Yep Started with His Own Roots," *Seattle Post-Intelligencer* (June 11, 2001). http://seattlepi.nwsource .com/books/26689_immigrant11 .shtml.

3 Yep, "I Have a Watch," p. 5.

4 Laurence Yep, *Dragon's Gate*. New York: HarperCollins, 1993, p. 93.

5 Ibid., p. 270.

6 Laurence Yep, "Paying with Shadows," *Lion and the Unicorn* 30, no. 2 (April 2006): p. 157.

7 Laurence Yep, *Hiroshima: A Novella*. New York: Scholastic, 1995, p. 20.

8 Ibid., p. 50.

Chapter 5

1 Quoted in "Laurence Yep's Interview Transcript," Scholastic Inc. http://books.scholastic .com/teachers/authorsandbooks/ authorstudies/authorhome.jsp? authorID=101&displayName= Interview%20Transcript.

2 Quoted in Leonard S. Marcus, ed., *Author Talk*. New York: Simon & Schuster, 2000, p. 101.

3 Quoted in "Laurence Yep's Interview Transcript," Scholastic.

4 Quoted in "Transcript From an Interview with Laurence Yep," Reading Rockets. www .readingrockets.org/books/ interview/yep/transcript.

5 Quoted in "Laurence Yep's Interview Transcript," Scholastic.

6 Quoted in Marcus, *Author Talk*. p. 101.

7 Ibid., p. 102.

8 Quoted in "Transcript from an Interview with Laurence Yep," Reading Rockets.

9 Ibid.

10 Quoted in "Laurence Yep's Interview Transcript," Scholastic.

Chapter 6

1 J.R.R. Tolkien, *The Hobbit.* Boston: Houghton Mifflin, 1997, p. 206.

2 Yep, "I Have a Watch," p. 9.

3 Quoted in "Laurence Yep's Interview Transcript," Scholastic.

4 Quoted in Johnson-Feelings, *Presenting Laurence Yep*, p. 17.

5 Ibid., p. 18.

6 Passage from *Dragon of the Lost Sea* reprinted in Johnson-Feelings, *Presenting Laurence Yep*, p. 5.

7 Quoted in Johnson-Feelings, *Presenting Laurence Yep*, p. 6.

8 Laurence Yep, *Seademons.* New York: Harper & Row, 1977, p. 1.

9 Laurence Yep, "The Outsider in Fiction and Fantasy," *English Journal* 94, no. 3 (January 2005): p. 52.

10 Laurence Yep, *The Imp That Ate My Homework.* New York: HarperCollins, 1998, p. 71.

Chapter 7

1 Laurence Yep, *The Mark Twain Murders.* New York: Four Winds Press, 1982, p. 55.

2 Ibid., p. 72.

3 Mark Twain, *Roughing It.* Library of the University of Virginia. Chapter 54, p. 391. http://etext.lib.virginia.edu/toc/modeng/public/TwaRoug.html.

4 Ibid.

5 Passage from *The Tom Sawyer Fires*, reprinted in Johnson-Feelings, *Presenting Laurence Yep*, pp. 50–51.

6 Laurence Yep, *The Case of the Goblin Pearls.* New York: HarperCollins, 1997, p. 7.

7 Ibid., pp. 133–134.

8 Ibid., p. x.

Chapter 8

1 Laurence Yep, *Angelfish.* New York: G.P. Putnam's Sons, 2001, p. 120.

2 Ibid., p. 217.

3 Laurence Yep, *Ribbons.* New York: G.P. Putnam's Sons, 1992, p. 108.

4 Laurence Yep, *The Cook's Family.* New York: G.P. Putnam's Sons, 1998, p. 14.

5 Laurence Yep, *The Amah.* New York: G.P. Putnam's Sons, 1999, p. 59.

6 Passage from *Kind Hearts and Gentle Monsters*, reprinted in Johnson-Feelings, *Presenting Laurence Yep*, p. 56.

7 Yep, *The Lost Garden*, p. 107.

8 Passage from *Kind Hearts and Gentle Monsters*, reprinted in Johnson-Feelings, *Presenting Laurence Yep*, p. 54.

Chapter 9

1 Yep, "I Have a Watch," p. 7.

2 Laurence Yep, *The Tiger's Apprentice.* New York: HarperCollins, 2003, p. 4.

3 Ibid., p. 183.

4 Yep, "I Have a Watch," p. 7.

5 Quoted in David Rooney, "M'max Traps Tiger," Variety.com. www .variety.com/article/VR111788208 9?categoryid=13&cs=1.

6 "Author Laurence Yep Wins 2005 Wilder Award," news release, American Library Association. www.ala .org/ala/pressreleases2005a/ 2005wilderwinner.htm.

7 Laurence Yep, "Wilder Medal Acceptance," *Horn Book* 81, no. 4 (July–August 2005): p. 429.

8 Laurence Yep, *The Earth Dragon Awakes: The San Francisco Earthquake of 1906.* New York: HarperCollins, 2006, p. 20.

9 Quoted in Bonnie O'Brian, "Meet Laurence Yep," California Readers. www.californiareaders .org/interviews/yep_laurence .html.

10 "Author Laurence Yep Wins 2005 Wilder Award," American Library Association.

WORKS BY LAURENCE YEP

Books

1973 *Sweetwater*

1975 *Dragonwings*

1977 *Child of the Owl*; *Seademons*

1979 *Sea Glass*

1980 *Green Darkness*

1982 *Kind Hearts and Gentle Monsters*; *The Mark Twain Murders*; *Dragon of the Lost Sea*

1983 *Liar, Liar*

1984 *The Serpent's Children*; *The Tom Sawyer Fires*

1985 *Dragon Steel*; *Mountain Light*; *The Shadow Lord*

1986 *Monster Makers, Inc.*

1987 *Curse of the Squirrel*

1989 *The Rainbow People*

1990 *Dragon Cauldron*; *When the Bomb Dropped: The Story of Hiroshima*

1991 *The Lost Garden*; *The Star Fisher*; *Tongues of Jade*

1992 *Dragon War*; *Ribbons*; *American Dragons: A Collection of Asian American Voices* (editor)

1993 *Butterfly Boy*; *Dragon's Gate*; *The Shell Woman and the King*; *The Man Who Tricked a Ghost*

1994 *Ghost Fox*; *The Tiger Woman*; *The Boy Who Swallowed Snakes*; *The Junior Thunder Lord*; *Foxfire*

1995 *Hiroshima: A Novella*; *Later, Gator*; *Tree of Dreams: Ten Tales from the Garden of Night*; *Thief of Hearts*; *The City of Dragons*

1997 *The Khan's Daughter: A Mongolian Folktale*; *The Dragon Prince: A Chinese Beauty and the Beast Tale*; *The Case of the Goblin Pearls*

1998 *The Imp That Ate My Homework*; *The Cook's Family*; *The Case of the Lion Dance*

1999 *The Amah*; *The Case of the Fireworks*

2000 *The Journal of Wong Ming-Chung. A Chinese Miner: California, 1852*; *The Magic Paintbrush*; *Cockroach Cooties*; *Dream Soul*

2001 *Angelfish*; *The House of Light*; *Lady Ch'iao Kuo: The Red Bird of the South*

2002 *Spring Pearl: The Last Flower*

2003 *Skunk Scout*; *The Tiger's Apprentice*; *The Traitor*

2006 *Tiger's Blood*; *Tiger Magic*; *The Earth Dragon Awakes: The San Francisco Earthquake of 1906*

2007 *Dragon Road*

Plays

1987 *Pay the Chinaman*; *Fairy Bones*; *Age of Wonders*

POPULAR BOOKS

THE AMAH

When ballet student Amy Chin's father dies, her mother takes a job as an *amah*, or nanny. Since her mother must work now, Amy must give up her dance lessons so that she has time to take care of her younger brothers and sisters.

ANGELFISH

Ballet student Robin Lee does not like her boss, the grumpy tropical fish store owner Mr. Cao. Then Robin learns his secret: Mr. Cao was a talented ballet star in China until his career was ended by the Cultural Revolution, the tumultuous period of Chinese history in which many talented people were jailed, tortured, and kicked out of the country.

THE CASE OF THE GOBLIN PEARLS

Lily Lew and her aunt, the actress Tiger Lil, team up to tackle a mystery in Chinatown: Who stole the priceless pearls from the Happy Fortune sweatshop? Along the way, Lily learns about the sacrifices made by Chinese-American actors and actresses, and sees the deplorable working conditions for Chinese women who work in sweatshops.

CHILD OF THE OWL

One of the books of the Golden Mountain Chronicles series, Casey Young has to move in with her Chinese-American family members after her gambler father gets sick. Casey resists the move, but she soon grows close to her family when she learns about Chinese culture.

THE COOK'S FAMILY

Robin Lee returns in this book about a lonely cook in a Chinese restaurant who believes Robin is his daughter. Robin plays the part to humor the old man, but she also finds that she cherishes her time with him because of her family troubles at home.

DRAGON OF THE LOST SEA

In the first of four books that chronicles the adventures of the dragon Shimmer and her ally, a young boy named Thorn, the two team up to battle the evil witch Civet and return the Inland Sea to its rightful owners, the dragon clan.

DRAGON'S GATE

Part of the Golden Mountain Chronicles, the book tells the story of Chinese immigrant Otter who arrives in California in 1867, where he works to build the transcontinental railroad. In China, Otter was a member of a wealthy and prominent family, but in California he is just another worker.

DRAGONWINGS

Perhaps Laurence Yep's most critically acclaimed book, *Dragon-wings* is the fictional account of the efforts of immigrant aviator Fung Joe Guey to build and fly an airplane during the era in which Wilbur and Orville Wright also experimented with powered flight.

THE EARTH DRAGON AWAKES: THE SAN FRANCISCO EARTHQUAKE OF 1906

Yep's story about the 1906 earthquake and fire that leveled San Francisco is told through the eyes of two boys: Henry Travis, the son of a wealthy San Francisco family, and Chin, the son of the Travis family's houseboy.

HIROSHIMA: A NOVELLA

The story of the atomic bombing of Hiroshima at the conclusion of World War II does not stop with the devastation of the city and its people. Yep continues the story to describe the "Hiroshima Maidens," the disfigured women whom American surgeons helped after the war.

KIND HEARTS AND GENTLE MONSTERS

The book tells the story of a teenage romance with an unusual twist: Charlie is the athlete and good student; Chris (a young woman) is the troublemaker. It is Chris who tries to convince Charlie to stop being so rigid in his ways.

THE MARK TWAIN MURDERS

Before he became a novelist, Mark Twain worked as a reporter for a San Francisco newspaper. In this story, he teams up with a street waif named Duke Dougherty to solve the murder of Duke's father.

RIBBONS

Robin Lee does not get along with her grandmother until she surprises her one day and discovers she is a victim of the Chinese custom of "foot binding," which has made her a cripple.

THE SERPENT'S CHILDREN

The first book in the Golden Mountain Chronicles begins as the family of Cassia Young joins the Taiping Rebellion in 1849; Yep based the story in part on his own family's experiences in nineteenth-century China.

THE STAR FISHER

Yep based the saga of the Lee family on his own mother's arrival in Clarksburg, West Virginia, where her father went into the laundry business. The main character, a young girl named Joan Lee, is proud of her race and heritage and stands up to prejudice.

SWEETWATER

In Yep's first book, the Silkies and Mainlanders are stranded on the planet Harmony, where both groups are suspicious of one another. The book features the plight of Tyree, a Silkie who must find a way to adjust to the new culture he finds on Harmony.

THE TIGER'S APPRENTICE

This is the first of a three-book series about Mr. Hu, the shape-shifting magical tiger, and Tom, a young Chinese-American boy. Tom helps Mr. Hu guard the precious phoenix egg from the evil Kung Kung, who seeks to steal the egg and use it to throw the Earth into turmoil.

POPULAR CHARACTERS

AMY CHIN

Amy Chin must give up ballet lessons after her father dies. She soon finds herself an outcast in her own family as her mother, brothers, and sisters lavish affection on Stephanie, the young girl whom Amy's mother is paid to take care of.

CASEY AND STACY YOUNG

Cassia Young's distant descendant, Casey, grows up in the Chinatown of the 1960s. In *Child of the Owl*, Casey learns about Chinese culture from her grandmother Paw-Paw. In the book's sequel, *Thief of Hearts*, Paw-Paw and Casey's daughter, Stacy, defend a Chinese immigrant girl accused of theft.

CASSIA YOUNG

Cassia is the main character in the first two books in the Golden Mountain Chronicles: *The Serpent's Children* and *Mountain Light*. In *The Serpent's Children*, Cassia's family endures the horrors of the Taiping Rebellion, in which some 20 million Chinese died.

DUKE DOUGHERTY

Duke Dougherty is a homeless San Francisco street waif who believes he is descended from royalty and prefers to be called "His Grace, the Duke of Baywater." In *The Mark Twain Murders* and *The Tom Sawyer Fires*, he teams up with newspaper reporter Mark Twain to solve crimes in 1860s San Francisco.

JOAN LEE

The featured character of *The Star Fisher*, Joan and her family move to Clarksburg, West Virginia, where she found herself one of the few Asian faces in the small town. Yep based Joan on his mother, Franche Lee

LILY LEW

Lily Lew and her aunt, former movie actress Tiger Lil, team up to solve crimes in San Francisco's Chinatown in several books: *The Case of the Goblin Pearls*; *The Case of the Lion Dance*; and *The Case of the Firecrackers*.

MOON SHADOW

In *Dragonwings*, young Moon Shadow meets Windrider, the father he never knew, at Angel Island. Together, they follow Windrider's dream to build and fly an engine-powered airplane.

OTTER

In *Dragon's Gate*, the adopted son of Cassia Young leaves a comfortable home and family life in China to immigrate to America; when he arrives, he is recruited to build the transcontinental railroad. Otter returns in the sequel, *The Traitor*, where he finds himself caught up in the 1885 miners' riot in Rock Springs, Wyoming.

ROBIN LEE

Ballet student Robin Lee is the featured character in *Ribbons*; *The Cook's Family*; and *Angelfish*. In the course of the three stories, she learns a lot about her family and Chinese culture, such as the horrific practice of "foot binding," the terrible years of the Cultural Revolution, and the problems of Chinese immigrants forced to leave their families behind.

SACHI

Sachi is a young girl living in Hiroshima, Japan, when the U.S. Air Force drops the atomic bomb on the city to end World War II. Burned and disfigured by the blast, Sachi becomes one of the "Hiroshima Maidens" who receives reconstructive surgery in the United States after the war.

THORN

Thorn befriends Shimmer, the dragon whose ocean has been stolen by the witch in *Dragon of the Lost Sea*. Thorn and Shimmer team up to return the ocean to the dragon clan. Their adventures continue in three sequels: *Dragon Steel*; *Dragon Cauldron*; and *Dragon War*.

TOM

Tom is the reluctant apprentice to Mr. Hu, the magical shape-shifting tiger. Mr. Hu serves as a Guardian over the phoenix egg, whose powers can be used to destroy the Earth. Tom accompanies Mr. Hu in three adventures: *The Tiger's Apprentice*; *Tiger's Blood*; and *Tiger Magic*.

TYREE

The main character in *Sweetwater*, Tyree is a Silkie, an alien on the planet Harmony. Silkies have learned to find drinkable water below the surface of the doomed planet.

MAJOR AWARDS

1975 *Dragonwings* selected *New York Times* Outstanding Book of the Year.

1976 *Dragonwings* selected by the American Library Association as a Newbery Honor Book; the International Reading Association for the Children's Book Award; and the National Council of Social Studies for the Carter A. Woodson Award.

1977 *Child of the Owl* selected for *Boston Globe-Horn Book* Award; *School Library Journal* Best Books for Spring; and the *New York Times* Outstanding Book of the Year.

1978 *Child of the Owl* selected by the Women's International League for Peace and Freedom for the Jane Addams Award.

1979 *Dragonwings* selected for the University of Wisconsin Lewis Carroll Shelf Award; *Sea Glass* selected for the Commonwealth Club of California Silver Medal.

1980 *Dragonwings* selected for the New York Public Library's Books for the Teen Age.

1984 *Dragonwings* selected for the Friend of Children and Literature Award.

1986 *Dragon Steel* selected for Child Study Association of America Children's Books of the Year.

1989 *The Rainbow People* selected for the *Boston Globe-Horn Book* Award.

1990 Laurence Yep awarded a fellowship by the National Endowment for the Arts.

1993 *Dragon's Gate* selected as a Newbery Honor Book.

2005 Laurence Yep selected for Laura Ingalls Wilder Award.

BIBLIOGRAPHY

Books

Dear, Pamela S., ed. *Contemporary Authors: New Revision Series*, vol. 46. Detroit, Mich.: Gale Research, 1995.

Johnson-Feelings, Diane. *Presenting Laurence Yep*. New York: Twayne, 1995.

Olendorg, Donna, ed. *Something About the Author*, vol. 69. Detroit, Mich.: Gale Research, 1992.

Peacock, Scot, ed. *Something About the Author*, vol. 123. Farmington Hills, Mich.: Gale Group, 2001.

————. *Contemporary Authors New Revision Series*: vol. 92. Farmington Hills, Mich.: Thomson Gale, 2001.

Marcus, Leonard S., ed. *Author Talk*. New York: Simon & Schuster, 2000.

Norton, Donna E. *Through the Eyes of a Child: An Introduction to Children's Literature*. Columbus, Ohio: Charles E. Merrill, 1983.

Tolkien, J.R.R. *The Hobbit*. Boston: Houghton Mifflin Co., 1997.

Yep, Laurence. *The Amah*. New York: G.P. Putnam's Sons, 1999.

————. *Angelfish*. New York: G.P. Putnam's Sons, 2001.

————. *The Case of the Goblin Pearls*. New York: HarperCollins, 1997.

————. *The Cook's Family*. New York: G.P. Putnam's Sons, 1998.

————. *Dragon's Gate*. New York: HarperCollins, 1993.

————. *Dragonwings*. New York: Scholastic, 1975.

————. *The Earth Dragon Awakes: The San Francisco Earthquake of 1906*. New York: HarperCollins, 2006.

————. *Hiroshima: A Novella*. New York: Scholastic, 1995.

————. *The Lost Garden*. New York: Julian Messner, 1991.

————. *The Mark Twain Murders*. New York: Four Winds Press, 1982.

————. *Ribbons*. New York: G.P. Putnam's Sons, 1992.

————. *Seademons*. New York: Harper & Row, 1977.

————. *The Star Fisher*. New York: Morrow Junior Books, 1991.

————. *The Tiger's Apprentice*. New York: HarperCollins, 2003.

Periodicals

Goodnow, Cecelia. "For Inspiration, Yep Started With His Own Roots." *Seattle Post-Intelligencer*, June 11, 2001.

Marcus, Leonard S. "Talking With Authors." *Publishers Weekly* 247, no. 7 (February 14, 2000): p. 98.

Ryder, Joanne. "Laurence Yep." *Horn Book* 81, no. 4 (July–August 2005): p. 433.

Yep, Laurence. "The Outsider in Fiction and Fantasy." *English Journal* 94, no. 3 (January 2005): p. 52.

———. "Paying With Shadows." *Lion and the Unicorn* 30, no. 2 (April 2006): p. 157.

———. "True Heroes." *Horn Book Magazine* 78, no. 6 (November– December 2002): p. 792.

———. "Wilder Medal Acceptance." *Horn Book* 81, no. 4 (July– August 2005): p. 429.

Other Sources

"Author Laurence Yep Wins 2005 Wilder Award," American Library Association. Available online. URL: http://www.ala.org/ala/ pressreleases2005a/2005wilderwinner.htm.

Laurence Yep's Hyperion Books for Children Biography. Available online. URL: http://www.hyperionbooksforchildren.com/authors/displayAI .asp?id=191&ai=a.

"Laurence Yep's Interview Transcript," Scholastic Inc. Available online. URL: http://content.scholastic.com/browse/contributor.jsp?id=1229.

HarperCollins interview with Laurence Yep about *The Traitor*. Available online. URL: http://www.harpercollins.com/authorintro/index .asp?authorid=12929.

O'Brian, Bonnie. "Meet Laurence Yep," California Readers. Available online. URL: http://www.californiareaders.org/interviews/yep_ laurence.html.

Rooney, David. "M'max Traps Tiger," Variety.com. Available online. URL: http://www.variety.com/article/VR1117882089?categoryid=13&cs=1.

"Transcript From an Interview With Laurence Yep," Reading Rockets. Available online. URL: http://www.readingrockets.org/books/ interview/yep/transcript.

Yep, Laurence. "I Have a Watch," speech given at the University of California–Davis School of Education, January 19, 2005.

FURTHER READING

Ambrose, Stephen E. *Nothing Like It in the World: The Men Who Built the Transcontinental Railroad, 1863–1869*. New York: Simon & Schuster, 2001.

Baker, Rodney. *Hiroshima Maidens*. New York: Viking, 1985.

Barker, Malcolm E., ed. *Three Fearful Days: San Francisco Memoirs of the 1906 Earthquake and Fire*. San Francisco: Londonborn, 1998.

Clemens, Samuel Langhorne. *Clemens of the Call: Mark Twain in San Francisco*. Berkeley: University of California Press, 1969.

Hodges, Graham Russell. *Anna May Wong: From Laundryman's Daughter to Hollywood Legend*. New York: Palgrave Macmillan, 2004.

Lai, Him Mark, Genny Lim, and Judy Yung. *Island: Poetry and History of Chinese Immigrants on Angel Island, 1910–1940*. Seattle: University of Washington Press, 1999.

Norton, Andre. *Witch World*. Boston: G.K. Hall, 1977.

Storti, Craig. *Incident at Bitter Creek: The Story of the Rock Springs Chinese Massacre*. Ames, Iowa: Iowa State Press, 1990.

Thompson, Ruth Plumly. *The Pirates in Oz*. New York: Del Rey, 1986.

Yung, Judy, Gordon Chang, and Him Mark Lai, eds. *Chinese American Voices: From the Gold Rush to the Present*. Berkeley: University of California Press, 2006.

Web Sites

Laura Ingalls Wilder Medal Winners
www.ala.org/ala/alsc/awardsscholarships/literaryawds/wildermedal/wildermedal.htm

"Learning About Laurence Yep," Rutgers University School of Communication, Information and Library Studies
www.scils.rutgers.edu/~kvander/yep.html

Science Fiction and Fantasy Writers of America
www.sfwa.org

Virtual Museum of the City of San Francisco
www.sfmuseum.org

PICTURE CREDITS

INDEX

130

ABOUT THE AUTHOR

HAL MARCOVITZ is a writer based in Chalfont, Pennsylvania. His other books in the series include biographies of Bruce Coville, R.L. Stine, Will Hobbs, Maurice Sendak, Scott O'Dell, and Pat Mora.